COOKERY
HINTS

COOKERY
HINTS

Random Little Library
an imprint of
Random House Australia Pty Ltd
20 Alfred Street, Milsons Point NSW 2061

Sydney Melbourne London New York
Auckland Johannesburg
and agencies throughout the world

Series Co-ordination: Gordon Cheers
Design: Liz Nicholson, Design Bite
Typeset by Axiom, 139 Charles Street, Abbotsford Vic 3067

ISBN 0 09 182805 8

CONTENTS

INGREDIENTS
AND LARDER

In most households the kitchen is an important centre of activity, so make sure your cooking area is well lit above the workbenches, tables and stove. Windows do not provide enough ventilation as they are often closed, so you should have a fan above the stove or in the ceiling. Rubbish should be disposed of in a small closable bin which can be emptied into your outside bin.

Keep your sink, stove and workbench or table near to each other. Storage cupboards with frequently required items such as flour, sugar and cooking oil should be near the work area. Store small items in high cupboards, heavier foodstuffs in low cupboards. Kitchen cutlery and utensils such as knives and peelers must be near the workbench.

Don't have your refrigerator too near the stove. Choose a refrigerator that suits the needs of your household and the sort of catering you plan to do. Will you need more freezing space than is provided in a conventional upright refrigerator? You may need a double-door combined refrigerator/freezer, or perhaps a separate freezer.

In this chapter you will find explanations of cooking terms, suggestions on storage and kitchen utensils and tips on the herbs and flavourings that should be part of your culinary equipment.

Accompaniment

A sauce or food that traditionally accompanies another food.

Aerating or raising agents

Raising agents are various substances added to mixtures before cooking to make food rise under the influence of heat.

Air is a natural raising agent as it expands during cooking. Other raising agents are baking powder, cream of tartar, bicarbonate of soda and yeast. Self-raising flour contains a raising agent.

If your raising agent contains cream of tartar, you must cook the mixture as soon as moisture is added, as this combination causes the agent to start its work.

If you use a phosphate aerator, the food can be allowed to stand for a time as it is heat, rather than moisture, which will cause it to work.

Aspic

Aspic is a clear savoury jelly in which food is presented. It is usually made from a meat or vegetable stock with added gelatin and formed in a mould.

Au gratin

Au gratin describes a dish covered with sauce and breadcrumbs or grated cheese which is then browned in the oven or under the griller.

The dish does not have to contain cheese — although it often does.

Bacon

Keep your bacon rinds when you cut them off.

If you crisp them in the oven for 10-15 minutes they will make a delicious garnish for soups and salads.

Bain marie

A bain marie is a heatproof dish containing hot water. You cook a custard in the oven by standing the dish in a bain marie. You make hollandaise or béarnaise sauce in a saucepan in a bain marie. This method of cooking avoids direct heat overcooking delicate egg-based sauces and causing them to curdle.

Baking blind

To bake blind means to cook a pastry case without filling. Line a pie pan with pastry, cut some greaseproof paper to line the insides and sides of the pastry, then fill bottom with rice or beans and cook for the specified time.

Basic kitchen utensils

In your kitchen you should have a cake cooler, cake pans, can opener, large chopper, at least one wooden chopping board, plastic or metal colander, corkscrew, egg lifter, egg slicer, flour sifter, frying pan or wok, funnels, garlic press, grater, hand or electric beater, juice squeezer, kitchen scissors, knives (including bread, carving and paring knives), metal skewers, metric measures, mixing bowls, pastry brush, pepper mill, perforated spoon, potato masher, potato peeler, rolling pin, saucepans of different capacities, tongs, wire strainer, wire whisk and wooden spoon.

Basil

The most common variety of this aromatic annual herb is sweet basil. It is used as a garnish in salads and often with tomatoes. Pesto sauce, a pungent mixture of ground pine nuts, parmesan cheese, olive oil and basil, is served with pasta dishes.

Basil leaves should be torn rather than chopped for best flavour and aroma.

Basting

Basting is spooning liquid over food to keep it moist

during cooking. For example, roasting meat should be basted with the fat and juices several times during cooking. Barbecuing meats should be basted with juices or marinade.

Bay leaves

Bay leaves are used dry or fresh to flavour sauces and casseroles and in stock making.

Try tucking a bay leaf inside a split potato before baking it in its jacket. The bay leaf gives it a delicious flavour.

Scatter bay leaves in your kitchen cupboards to discourage insect pests.

Beating

Beating is the process of aerating a mixture by turning it over and over in a circular motion.

Never change direction when you are beating a mixture. This could reduce the air absorption process.

Blanching

Dip fruit and vegetables into boiling water for a minute to 'blanch' or partly cook them.

A delicious way to serve green vegetables such as beans or broccoli is to blanch them in boiling water, then plunge them into cold water for a second to restore their bright colour. The cooking is finished off by tossing them in hot butter (sautéeing) or stir-frying.

Blanch almonds in a bowl of boiling water. Their skins will expand and slide off easily.

Remove skins easily from tomatoes and peaches by blanching them in boiling water for a minute.

Blending
Blending is combining ingredients into a smooth paste.

You can use a food processor on low setting to blend ingredients, or you can blend with a wooden or metal spoon.

Boiling point
The boiling point, or when the surface of liquid is bubbling briskly, is 100°C for water.

Bouquet garni
A bouquet garni is a small bunch of herbs tied together and added to soups, sauces or casseroles for flavour.

After cooking the herbs are removed.

A bouquet garni is usually made up of a bay leaf, spring of parsley and either thyme, sage, marjoram or rosemary. Alter the composition to suit the dish.

Bread
Bread may be frozen to keep it. It keeps well for 3 or 4 days in the refrigerator, or for 2 or 3 days in a bread crock or tin. White bread goes stale faster than wholemeal.

Freeze cut loaves to keep them fresh. Just pull out a slice at a time as you need it.

Fresh bread is more easily cut if it is refrigerated first.

Stale bread can be freshened if you dip rolls under the cold tap for an instant or wipe the surface of bread over with a damp cloth and crisp in a warm oven for 10 minutes.

Use a warm knife to cut fresh bread.

Don't waste your stale bread. Break it into pieces and leave in the warm oven overnight when you have finished cooking. When the pieces have dried through, put them through the blender to make breadcrumbs.

Cayenne pepper

Made from hot chillies or capsicums, cayenne should be used sparingly in marinades, soups and Asian dishes. Don't get it near your eyes and wash your hands thoroughly after using it.

Cereals

Cereals are the edible seeds of grasses. These include wheat (flour, breakfast cereals, spaghetti), oats (oatmeal, rolled oats); rice and maize (sweet corn, cornflour and polenta).

Chives

Chives are delicately flavoured members of the onion family. They are easily grown in a pot and will last all year round in mild climates. Chives are delicious chopped in omelettes and salads, or sprinkled on soups or potatoes.

Slice a fresh tomato on hot buttered toast and sprinkle with chopped chives, salt and freshly ground black pepper.

Cinnamon
This is a strong spice — be careful not to use too much. It is excellent in cakes and fruit dishes.

Sprinkle cinnamon and sugar on hot buttered toast for a delicious snack.

Clarify
To purify or clean by removing sediments or impurities. Clarified butter

is the fatty portion of butter obtained by removing the non-fatty constituents.

Cloves
You can buy cloves whole or ground. Use them to flavour fruit dishes, especially baked and stewed apples and pears, and in milk puddings such as custard.

Oil of cloves will relieve toothache.

Use cloves in herb and lavender sachets to keep moths out of clothes cupboards.

Condiments
Condiments are highly flavoured spices, seasonings and sauces.

Consommé

Consommé is a clear thin soup: vegetable, chicken, meat or fish. It is made by reducing stock to concentrate the flavour.

Add a few strips of blanched vegetables to garnish a vegetable consommé and you have consommé julienne.

Coriander

Coriander is often called Chinese parsley and is used in Asian cooking in curries, soups and as a garnish. Add it towards the end of cooking.

It can be bought in bunches at greengrocers or grown in pots, and deserves to be better known.

Creaming

Creaming is the process of working butter or other shortening together with sugar into a fluffy cream.

You can use your hand (the warmth will help to melt the butter), a wooden spoon, or an electric blender.

Always cream butter at room temperature.

Croûtons

Fry small cubes of stale bread in hot butter or oil and scatter the crisp croûtons on the top of soups or salads.

Curry powder

A blend of spices including coriander, chillies, cumin, ginger, fenugreek, turmeric, ginger, cinnamon, nutmeg and cloves.

Use it to make curry, or to flavour soups, egg dishes and sauces.

Dice
To dice means to cut into cubes.

Dill
Dill is a leafy green plant. Its mild sweet flavour is excellent with fish.

If you can get fresh dill, use it to wrap fish when grilling or pan frying, or chop it and add to butter sauce or mayonnaise. It is good in potato salad.

Use the dried seeds or powder if no fresh dill is available.

Dredging
Dredging means sprinkling or rubbing meat or other food with flour, usually prior to browning, sealing or sautéeing it.

Fennel
Fennel is a leafy plant tasting of liquorice. It has a stronger flavour than dill. Use it in salads, with fish or chopped on boiled new potatoes.

Flour
Plain, self-raising and wholemeal are the types of flour most commonly used. During manufacture, raising agents are added to self-raising flour and wholemeal self-raising flour.

Self-raising flour contains either cream of tartar and bicarbonate of soda, or acid phosphate and bicarbonate of soda.

Flour is the basis of various mixtures to which raising agents are added to make them light, palatable and more easily digested, such as cakes, scones, bread and biscuits.

Folding

Folding is the process of combining two mixtures, one of which contains an aerating substance. Lie the lighter mixture on top of the heavier one and with a metal spoon, use a cutting action to fold the heavy mixture over the light one until they are blended.

Try not to overwork the mixture when folding. If you do, you'll lose the aerated quality.

Fruit and vegetable storage

Store all leafy green vegetables in plastic bags in the crisping compartment of the refrigerator.

Tubers such as potatoes and parsnips, onions and gourds such as pumpkin can be stored on wire racks in dark, ventilated cupboards. Do not store these in plastic bags.

Lemons may be stored in trays of sand for up to a year. Do not let them touch or overlap.

New potatoes do not keep longer than a week.

Don't store mushrooms in plastic bags — they will go slimy. Brown paper bags will allow them to breathe.

Store lettuce whole — they go brown if cut. They last better stored in paper bags than plastic.

Apples are best stored in the refrigerator after they have been in a controlled atmosphere store.

Cut the bottom off a stick of celery and stand it in a little water in the refrigerator to keep it fresh.

Don't store bananas in the refrigerator — they will go black.

To store the unused half of a cut avocado, leave the stone in the fruit, rub with lemon juice and cover

tightly with cling film. Store in the refrigerator.

Garlic

A pungent vegetable, garlic is universally used as a flavouring in meat, poultry and vegetable dishes and dressings.

When you are softening garlic in butter or oil, be careful that it doesn't burn as it will taste bitter.

Remember — a little garlic goes a long way.

Garlic keeps well in a cool dry atmosphere.

Remove the odour of garlic from your hands by rubbing with a cut lemon.

Garnish

Garnish is the decoration of trimming on food. Use

parsley, chives, dill or any green herb to garnish savoury dishes.

Ginger

Ginger is a pungent root and its spicy flavour in powdered form is good in cakes and puddings.

Use fresh ginger chopped in stir-fry dishes.

The Chinese use it in fish cookery as Westerners use lemon.

Glazing

In glazing, you brush the surface of food with sugar, milk or egg to give an attractive shiny appearance.

Your Christmas ham can be easily glazed with a brown sugar syrup. Lift off the skin and cover the outside with pineapple rings secured with toothpicks and paint the glaze over the top.

Groceries

Once grocery items such as tea, coffee, flour, sugar, cereals, rice, barley, pasta and biscuits have been opened, they should be stored in airtight and insect-proof containers.

Brown sugar will not go lumpy in the jar if you add a piece of lemon or orange peel.

Cooking oil should be stored in a dark cool place to avoid going rancid.

Don't keep olive oil near the stove.

If honey granulates during cold weather, stand the jar in hot water to restore the texture, or pop the jar in the microwave for a few seconds.

Herbs
Store fresh herbs in the refrigerator in plastic bags.

If you blanch herbs for 10 seconds in boiling water, then plunge them into cool water to refresh them, you can freeze them for future use in cooked dishes.

Wrap small quantities of herbs separately.

Horseradish
This is a small plant with a cream-coloured radish-like root. It has a strong, sharp flavour. Grate the root and use it to flavour sauce served with roast beef.

Infusion
This is the liquid obtained by standing a substance in boiling water.

Julienne
Julienne is a French term for the fine strips of cooked vegetables used to garnish thin soups and other dishes.

Kneading
Kneading is the process of working dough to a smooth consistency.

In making bread, kneading distributes the yeast evenly through the dough.

Lemon grass

Lemon grass is a fragrant herb used in Asian soups and curries.

Mace

Mace has a similar flavour to nutmeg but stronger. It's good with pumpkin soup.

Marjoram

A green herb, marjoram has a much better flavour fresh than dry. It is sweet and spicy.

Use it in salads and stuffings for meat, particularly lamb and veal.

It's also good chopped and sprinkled on boiled potatoes.

Measurement

Metric scales are an essential item in any kitchen.

A set of standard dry measuring cups ($^1/_4$, $^1/_3$, $^1/_2$, 1 cup) and standard spoons for dry and liquid measures are also useful.

You will also need a glass graduated measuring jug, preferably heatproof, measuring up to a litre for liquid measures.

Check liquid measures at eye level.

Remember that all measures given in recipes are level.

When you measure butter by the cup or spoon, it should be soft but *not* liquid.

Here are some useful equivalent measures.

Liquids	
1 teaspoon = 5 ml	½ cup = 125 ml or
2 teaspoons = 10 ml or	6 tablespoons
1 dessertspoon	¾ cup = 185 ml
2 dessertspoons =	1 cup = 250 ml
20 ml or 1 tablespoon	2 cups = 500 ml
¼ cup = 65 ml or	4 cups = 1 litre
3 tablespoons	

Solids	
1 tablespoon = 30 g butter,	1 cup sugar = 250 g
lard, margarine, salt or	2 tablespoons flour = 30 g
sugar	1 cup flour = 100 g
1 cup butter = 250 g	4 cups flour = 500 g

Oven temperatures	
Cool 100°C	Moderate 200°C
Slow 150°C	Hot 220°C

Mint
In a stuffing, sauce or jelly, mint is the classic accompaniment for roast lamb. Mint leaves scattered in cupboards and under carpets will discourage fleas and moths.

Mustard
The seeds of the mustard plant are ground and combined with various other ingredients to form pastes. English mustard is hotter than French, which contains vinegar.

Use mustard to accompany beef, in salad dressings and in sauces to go with salted and boiled meats.

Nutmeg
Grate nutmeg into milk puddings and fruit dishes.

Add a sprinkle to mashed potato or to pasta dishes.

Nutrient
A nutrient is a component of food that contributes to bodily function in order to support life, such as carbohydrates, protein, fat, vitamins, minerals, fibre and water.

Oregano
Oregano is a relation of marjoram but has a stronger flavour. Use it in stuffing for roast lamb and veal, and in green salads.

Parboiling
Parboiling is the process of partly cooking by boiling. Cooking is then completed by another method.

Parboil potatoes before frying or roasting for a crisp finish.

Parsley
The best known and most widely used herb, parsley can be grown all the year round in mild climates. Use it in salads, sauces, stuffing, soups and as a garnish.

Fry parsley heads in oil to accompany fish, or add it to butter as a sauce.

Chew parsley to sweeten your breath. Remember parsley stalks have an intense flavour. Use them to flavour dishes where appearance isn't important.

Pepper
Pepper is the hot powder ground from peppercorns that is used as a flavouring and stimulant to the taste buds. White pepper is not as strong as black.

Black pepper should be ground as you need it as it loses its flavour quickly.

Pimento
Pimento berries are used whole or ground for pickles, meat dishes, stock and fruit puddings. Pimento combines the flavour of cloves, nutmeg and cinnamon.

Purée
Purée is a fine pulp obtained by pushing food through a sieve or using an electric blender.

Reducing
Reducing means boiling stock or a mixture in an

open saucepan to reduce the amount of water it contains and so increase the flavour and concentration.

Refrigerator storage

Keep meat, fish, poultry and dairy products such as butter, cheese and milk in the refrigerator.

Cooked food should be covered with cling wrap or placed in a container with a lid and stored in the refrigerator after it has reached room temperature.

Never put warm food in the refrigerator. It will cause odour and overload the cooling system.

If your refrigerator smells, wipe it out with vinegar and water or bicarbonate of soda and water solution.

Once frozen food has defrosted, do not refreeze it.

All food kept in the refrigerator should be covered — with the exception of eggs. Food not covered will dry out and may smell unpleasant.

Never wash eggs before storing. This destroys their natural protective seal.

Do not keep fish longer than two days in the refrigerator. If you wish to store it for longer it should be frozen immediately after purchase — but *not* if it has been frozen before.

Do not wrap fish in plastic — it may cause it to exude

moisture. Cover it with foil or put it in a container.

Red meat should be wrapped in plastic or freezer bags and kept in the meat compartment. If fresh when bought, it should last up to a week.

Poultry should be wiped and then stored in a plastic bag in the meatkeeper. Do not keep poultry longer than two days before cooking.

If you wish to keep poultry longer, it should be frozen — but if it is already frozen, do *not* allow it to thaw.

Butter and margarine should be kept in their own compartment once unwrapped. Butter picks up smells and flavours easily.

Rigid plastic take-away food containers with lids are ideal for storing leftovers in the refrigerator.

Rosemary
Use sweet-smelling rosemary leaves to flavour baked fish and roast lamb.

Roux
A roux is a mixture of fat or butter and flour, blended together and cooked for a minute or two to bind it.

Use a roux to thicken sauces, gravies and casseroles.

Saffron
An expensive spice, saffron is used in small quantities

to flavour and colour fish and rice dishes.

Don't spill saffron on your clothes — it is a dye and will stain.

Sage
Use sage fresh or dry in stuffing for pork, game and poultry. It is also good with tomatoes.

Searing
Searing is browning the outside of meat very quickly over a hot flame to seal in the juices.

Sear meat or chicken before casseroling; sear meat on both sides when grilling or barbecuing.

Sesame
Sesame seeds are used to coat food before frying, or to flavour stir-fry and fish dishes.

Sesame oil is a tasty cooking alternative to olive or peanut oil.

Shortening
Shortening is the culinary term for fat, lard, dripping, butter, margarine, suet and vegetable oils.

Sifting
To sift is to use a strainer or sieve to remove lumps, incorporate air and mix ingredients thoroughly.

Stock
Stock is the liquid obtained by simmering bones or meat, vegetables and seasoning for several hours.

Stock is the basis of all good soups and sauces, and adds flavour to casseroles and gravies.

Sugars

Sugars are sweetening substances. These include brown sugar, raw sugar, coffee crystals, granulated or white sugar, caster sugar, icing sugar, loaf sugar, molasses, treacle and honey.

Tarragon

A fragrant herb, tarragon is delicious in stuffing for poultry and in herb vinegar. Add it to butter sauce for fish and vegetables. It gives the distinctive flavour to béarnaise sauce.

Thyme

There are several varieties of thyme, including lemon thyme.

Use it in stuffings for meat and poultry, salads and soups or chopped on cooked vegetables.

Add lemon thyme to the water when poaching a chicken.

Vanilla

The bean of the vanilla plant can be used whole or in essence to flavour milk puddings, milk drinks, cakes and biscuits.

Vanilla pods scattered around your cupboards make good cockroach repellents.

TIPS AND TECHNIQUES

In this chapter you will find hints on various cooking techniques: boiling, braising, frying, grilling, steaming and roasting, and some simple examples of each technique. Baking is discussed in the chapter on cakes and pastry.

Your basic cooking tool is some form of oven — with thermostat — and a cooking top. This means that if you have a family, you will probably need a conventional oven to roast and casserole. If you can afford it, a microwave for quick meals, defrosting and reheating is a useful adjunct — and some ovens nowadays combine conventional and microwave functions in one.

Gas, electricity, oil or solid fuel? All have their advantages. Electricity is probably the cleanest form of energy and electric ovens have less temperature fluctuation. Gas offers instant temperature control and the direct flame for grilling and roasting and, in some areas, oil or solid fuel-burning stoves with their double ovens and spacious hot plate area are used to heat whole kitchen area as well as feeding the family.

You will need at least one frying pan (of good weight), a set of saucepans, a steamer, and casserole dishes either of cast iron, enamel, or heatproof glass. Extra electrical cooking appliances such as a deep fryer, frypan or slow cooking pot can be useful especially to those who might have limited access to conventional stoves or cooking facilities.

Boiling

In boiling, the food is completely covered with water or liquid and cooked in a saucepan or pot on top of the stove. The liquid is brought to a fast boil, then the heat is reduced and the liquid simmers throughout the cooking process.

Boiling meats

Meats suitable for boiling are corned or salted meats such as silverside or brisket, pumped lamb or mutton, pickled pork, ham and unsalted meats such as mutton or chicken.

It is sometimes wise to soak salt meat before boiling it to get rid of excess salt.

To boil meat, you will need a pan large enough to hold both the meat and enough water to cover it.

Wipe the meat first then place it in a large saucepan of warm water with a teaspoon of salt. (Do not add salt if you are cooking salted meat.) Bring to the boil, and remove any scum that rises to the surface. Add 1 teaspoon vinegar, 1 sliced onion, bay leaf, 2 cloves, 3 or 4 slices of carrot, 3 or 4 slices of parsnip and a few black peppercorns.

Bring to the boil again, then turn down and simmer for the suggested time or until tender when pierced with a skewer. A large chicken may take 1-1½ hours; joints of meat under 1.5 kg will take 2 hours; joints of meat over 1.5 kg will take 2½-3 hours.

Boiled chicken is good served with caper, onion or parsley sauce. Salt meat goes well with mustard or onion sauce. *See* the chapter on soups and sauces.

Boiling vegetables

Boiling is the most common cooking technique for all vegetables. If you boil vegetables rapidly in a small amount of water, their vitamin and mineral content will be preserved, as well as their flavour and colour.

Keep the cooking time to a minimum when boiling vegetables. The longer you boil them the more likely they are to lose nutritional value. Cook all green vegetables until barely tender.

Do not leave the lid on the saucepan when boiling green vegetables. They will loose their colour and flavour.

Braising

In this technique, meat is first quickly fried in a little butter or oil over a high heat to brown it, then it is slowly cooked over a bed of vegetables with a little added stock in a casserole dish with a tightly fitting lid.

You can use any type of meat for a braised dish.

To vary braised dishes, add a little red wine as a substitute for some of the stock.

Here is a recipe for a simple braised beef to feed six.

Preheat the oven to 175°C. Lightly fry a couple of rashers of chopped bacon in a little butter in a heavy pan, then add 1 large sliced onion, 1 sliced carrot and 1 stalk of celery, 1 bay leaf, some herbs, salt and black peppercorns and fry for a few more minutes.

Put the vegetables into a heavy casserole. Flour a 2-kg piece of topside beef and lightly brown in a little butter in a heavy pan until sealed on all sides.

Put the meat on top of the vegetable base in the casserole, pour over 1½ cups stock, adjust seasoning, cover with a lid and cook in the oven for about 40-50 minutes.

Braising vegetables

Braising is also used as a technique to cook vegetables. Simply fry a couple of rashers of chopped bacon in a heavy saucepan, add the vegetables (green, yellow or white), season, add a little stock or water to cover and cook until tender with the lid on the saucepan.

Carving

Carving is a matter of practice and common sense that will be greatly helped by a very sharp knife or electric knife.

Carving beef

For beef, place the thickest end on your left with the undercut underneath. Lift the joint and turn, bringing the undercut to the front. Cut the undercut downward towards the bone on a slight angle in thick slices. Carve the upper part parallel with the ribs in long slices.

A round of beef should be cut in thin slices.

Carving lamb and pork

With lamb or pork, start with the small end of the leg on your left with the thick part to the far side of the dish. Insert a fork in the thickest part and lift the joint slightly towards you. Starting in the thickest part, cut medium slices down toward the bone.

Remove the crackling from pork before carving.

Carving chicken

Remove all trussing equipment from chickens before carving.

Place the chicken breast up on a carving board and have a plate close at hand to hold the pieces. Pierce the chicken firmly with a carving fork then, with a sharp knife, cut the skin between the leg and breast. Ease the knife into the leg joint at the back and cut through the thigh joint to remove the whole leg from the body. Cut through the joint to separate the drumstick and thigh.

Place the fork into the breast near the breastbone and cut off the wing. Slice the whole meat from the top of the breastbone and cut down toward the wing joint.

Casseroling

Meat is first floured and lightly browned in butter, then slowly cooked in a casserole dish in vegetables, wine and stock. You can use cheaper cuts of beef or lamb, poultry pieces or small whole birds.

The pieces of meat must be approximately the same size so that cooking will be even.

Remember it is the combination of fast browning, then long slow cooking (to develop the flavour and tenderise the meat), that makes a successful casserole.

Use veal or lamb shanks sawn across to make this classic osso bucco. Preheat oven to 200°C. Take 1.5 kg shanks, roll in a little plain flour, salt and black pepper. Brown shanks and a sliced onion in olive oil over a high heat. Place meat and onion in a casserole, add 1½ tablespoons tomato paste, 1 crushed clove garlic, 2 cups stock and a little white wine if desired.

Adjust seasoning to taste, cover with a tight-fitting lid, place in the hot oven, reduce heat then simmer on 150°C for 1½ hours. To serve, sprinkle with lemon rind and parsley.

This same procedure can be followed for stewing, except the meat is cooked on the stove top. Cover the saucepan tightly and cook on a low heat until tender.

Frying

Frying is a fast cooking process in which oil, butter, margarine or lard are raised to a high temperature in a pan or deep fryer. Portions of food are cooked in it for a short time to obtain a crisp and appetising finish.

All fats should be heated slowly so that an even temperature is reached throughout. If this is not done the fat at the bottom of the pan may burn.

When frying, avoid immersing food in the fat for too long. It should not become saturated with the fat so that the end result is greasy and unhealthy.

Before food is cooked in fats you should dry it thoroughly or coat it with flour, egg and breadcrumbs or batter. This will stop moisture seeping into the fat which will cause it to spit, and will prevent the food absorbing the cooking fat.

Breadcrumbs will stick better to cutlets, fish fillets and veal escalopes if you beat a dessertspoon of oil into each egg used for dipping.

Breadcrumb coatings are lighter if you add self-raising flour rather than plain flour to the coating mixture.

Foods cooked in oil or fat such as lard should be drained on absorbent paper to get rid of any excess.

Fried foods should be kept to a minimum. The principles of good nutrition emphasise that too much fat in the diet can increase the cholesterol level in the blood and therefore the risk of heart disease.

A non-stick frying pan is a good investment as it requires little or no greasing and will reduce the amount of fat needed in the frying process.

Remember that butter and margarine burn easily. If you are using them for frying, it is wise to add a little oil, as oil and lard have a higher burning point.

Frying — deep

You will need a deep saucepan and wire basket to lift out the food for deep frying. Potato chips and battered or crumbed foods such as fish and fritters are cooked this way.

Fat in a deep fryer can burst into flames spontaneously. Watch it at all times and keep a heavy wool blanket nearby when frying.

Foods should be coated with batter or egg and breadcrumbs before deep frying. Make a batter for fish and fritters by sifting 1/2 cup plain flour with a pinch of salt. Add an egg and

gradually stir in 7 tablespoons milk. Mix till quite smooth. Dip the food into the batter then allow excess batter to drip off before frying.

Heat the oil slowly until it gives off faint blue smoke and until a cube of bread sizzles when it is dipped in the oil. Lower the food into the fat in a wire basket and cook until golden brown. Lift out and drain on absorbent paper.

To cook perfect potato chips, peel and slice a good frying potato such as Desirée or patrone. Pat with a paper towel to draw off excess moisture. Heat oil or fat to blue smoke stage. Put the chips into the basket and lower into the deep fryer for 10 seconds only. Lift out and stand on absorbent paper for a minute, then reimmerse the chips into the hot fat and fry till golden brown. This double frying technique will result in crisp and delicious chips.

Frying — dry
Dry frying is suitable for food such as steak, chops or sausages that take time to cook through. Use just enough fat or butter to stop the food sticking to the pan, and don't have the heat too high or the food will burn.

Turn the food without piercing it to avoid loosing the juices — except for sausages which should be

pierced before cooking or they will burst.

Drain food after cooking to remove the excess fat.

Cook bacon this way but don't grease the pan at all as the fat will come from the bacon as it cooks. For crisp results press the bacon with your egg lifter and drain the fat off as it cooks.

Frying safely
If you are cooking on a gas stove, don't let the flame creep up the sides of the pan in case the fat catches fire.

Remember that water can make fat splatter and explode. Pat vegetables with paper towels before frying or roasting.

Strain your dripping after cooking and reuse — unless you have been frying fish.

If your fat catches fire, smother it with a heavy woollen blanket, lid, bicarbonate of soda or salt. Do not put water or flour on a fat fire: it will explode.

Keep used dripping and fat in a cool place.

Never put a lid on fat while you are heating it.

General rules

When preparing a meal, make sure that the dishes which take the longest to prepare and cook are dealt with first.

Read recipes carefully, noting ingredients, utensils and method before you start.

Collect ingredients on sheets of paper or plates or in basins. Measure as accurately as possible.

Collect all the utensils required.

Stack dirty utensils on the sink and put away packets of ingredients as soon as they are no longer needed.

Scrub chopping boards with cold water and abrasive cleaning powder, rinse and wipe dry with a dishcloth.

To get the maximum benefit from hot plates, use utensils that cover the surface of the plate and are perfectly flat.

Grilling

Grilling is a quick method of cooking small cuts of meat, poultry or fish using an open flame or dry heat. You can either cook over a fire (barbecue) or under a griller.

It is essential to have a high temperature to grill successfully. Preheat your griller to red hot and, if barbecuing, allow time to build a heat bank of glowing coals.

The heat must be maintained throughout the cooking.

Red meat and chicken must be seared on all sides first to seal in juices. Try to avoid breaking the surface of the meat (for example, with a fork) and thus letting out the juices. Always use tongs to turn the meat for this reason.

Sausages, however, should be pierced before grilling, or they will burst.

Meat for grilling should not be too thick (not more than 3.5 cm) so that it will cook through.

Grilling vegetables

Grilling is not a suitable cooking technique for vegetables as it dries them out. Exceptions are tomatoes and mushrooms if they are marinated in oil or brushed with butter first, and capsicums if you want to remove the skin.

Marinating

To avoid food drying out and to tenderise and add flavour while grilling or barbecuing, marinate meat for a couple of hours before cooking. Drain the meat to cook it, but use the marinade as a baste during grilling.

A typical marinade will contain oil and vinegar, wine or lemon juice and a variety of seasonings, herbs and spices. The oil will stop the food drying out and the vinegar will tenderise the meat.

Here is a basic simple marinade for red meat. Combine in a bowl 1 sliced onion, 1 clove of crushed garlic, $1/2$ cup olive oil, $1/2$ cup white vinegar, $1/4$ cup worcestershire sauce, $1/2$ cup tomato sauce or purée, salt, a handful of black peppercorns and a little sugar to taste. Soak the meat in this for at least 2 hours, then drain and grill or barbecue, basting frequently with the strained marinade.

Red wine makes an excellent marinade for beef and lamb. White wine is good for chicken, veal and pork.

Measuring techniques

All measures given in recipes are level.

When measuring a dry ingredient, lightly spoon it into the appropriate cup or spoon. Don't pack an ingredient tightly into a cup unless the recipe says to. Scrape off the excess with a spatula or knife, don't tap the cup.

For liquids, pour into the liquid measuring cup and check carefully at eye level for greater accuracy. Fill spoons to brimming.

To measure solids, spoon the ingredients lightly into a cup or spoon and level off with a knife or spatula.

To measure cheese in a cup, grate the cheese and then lightly pack it into the cup.

When measuring butter it should be soft but not liquid.

Poaching
Poached food is cooked in liquid, but it is not boiled.

The water or stock must not bubble and remains below boiling point throughout the cooking process.

In poaching, the food is not completely submerged in the water. The poaching liquid is used to baste the food.

For the perfect poached egg, bring a pan of water almost to boiling then turn right down so the water is not moving. Break an egg into a cup, then slide it gently into the water and leave for 5 minutes. If you like the yolk set, gently spoon a little water over it just before taking the egg from the water with an egg slice. A teaspoon of vinegar in the cooking water will

keep the white from dis-
integrating while poaching.

Pressure cooking

This is a method of cooking
whereby stews, meats and
vegetables are cooked in a
strong, closed cooking pan
above the normal boiling
point under pressure. It
results in shorter cooking
times, saving fuel, food
flavours and colours.
Because cooking is done
in a very small amount of
liquid and with no air in
the pan there is greater
vitamin and mineral
retention in the food.

Roasting

Roasting uses a hot oven to
roast meat, game or poultry
with accompanying
vegetables. Preheat the

oven to the required
temperature, place a
roasting pan with enough
dripping or fat in it to
generously cover the
bottom and melt the fat in
the oven.

First wipe the joint with
a damp cloth or paper
towels, then put it on a
rack over the dripping.
Baste the meat thoroughly
with the fat, season with
pepper and return to the
oven. Baste a couple of
times during cooking.

If you use high oven tem-
peratures (220°C) and a
short cooking time (say 30
minutes per kg) you will get
meat that is browned on
the outside and underdone
on the inside. A longer
cooking time at a lower

temperature will produce meat that is well cooked throughout.

Use the high temperature/ shorter cooking technique for roasting beef and lamb if you like it pink on the inside. Use a lower temperature for pork, veal, chicken and lamb if you like it cooked through.

When the roast is cooked, rest it in a warm place for 15 minutes before carving. Make the gravy and complete the cooking of vegetables during this time. As a general rule, remember that white meat should be cooked through.
Make sure your roasting pan is not too large for the size of the joint. If you leave too much space around the meat, the fat in the pan will overheat, splatter and smoke.

A roasting bag will help keep poultry moist and reduce the amount of fat necessary to roast. Sprinkle the inside of the bag with flour, puncture the bag and follow the manufacturer's directions for use.

French roasting is a variation of dry roasting that gives a special flavour. Proceed as for conventional roasting, but without a rack or dripping. Roast for 30 minutes in a moderate oven, then pour stock or wine over the joint and continue to cook, basting often. Skim any fat from the juices in the pan, drain, rest and serve.

Roasting temperatures

Here is a rough guide to cooking temperatures and times for roasting meat.

Use your own recipe book for more exact information. The books supplied by stove manufacturers are a good guide.

180°C *(Lower-temperature roasting)*	
Beef	40 minutes per kg
Lamb/mutton	60 minutes per kg
Veal	60 minutes per kg
Pork	60 minutes per kg
Stuffed meat	60 minutes per kg

220°C *(Higher-temperature roasting)*	
Beef	30 minutes per kg
Lamb/mutton	40 minutes per kg
Veal	50 minutes per kg
Pork	50 minutes per kg
Stuffed meats	50 minutes per kg

The lower-temperature method is better for pork, and for tougher cuts of meat, poultry, game and small roasts, as it does not dry out the meat as much.

Lower oven temperatures also mean less mess as the fat and liquids do not splatter as much.

Roasting vegetables

You can roast potatoes in the pan with the meat if you use the high-temperature method of roasting as the fat will be hot enough to make them crisp. Potatoes will take about an hour to roast, a little less if they are par-boiled first, so if your roast meat will take longer than this, add the potatoes at the appropriate time in the cooking.

If you are using low temperatures to cook your roast, do the potatoes in a separate pan on the higher shelf in the oven.

Safety tips

If food or liquid is spilt, clean it up immediately so you don't slip in it.

Put knives at the back of benches when young children are about.

Place saucepan handles to the sides of stoves, away from jets and passageways.

Lift the lids of saucepans away from you to allow steam to escape. Place hot lids upside down on a bench.

Never leave milk and fat unattended while being heated.

Don't use damp cloths to handle very hot equipment, as the moisture in the cloth can turn to steam and scald you.

When lighting gas jets, strike the match before turning on the gas.

Sautéeing

Sauter means to jump, and this frying technique involves tossing small pieces of food in butter, oil or fat so that they are just cooked without losing any flavour.

Do not overcrowd the pan when sautéeing — the food will stew instead of browning.

Sautéed food should not be drained after cooking.

Sautéeing is an excellent technique for cooking small pieces of green vegetables, such as sliced zucchinis or marrow, that don't need lengthy cooking. Pat vegetables with a paper towel before cooking to get rid of the moisture.

Steaming

In steaming, food is cooked in a container over a pan of boiling water. The hot steam cooks the food. It is a suitable cooking method for chicken, fish, shellfish and prawns, vegetables, and puddings such as steamed pudding.

Always replace the water in a steamer with boiling

water, so that no heat is lost and the cooking process is not interrupted.

You can improvise your own steamer by simply laying a plate across a saucepan of water.

Put the food to be steamed on the plate, cover with an upturned dish, and bring the water to the boil.

Stir-frying

Stir-frying is a quick and easy cooking technique that involves tossing small portions of meat, fish, chicken or vegetables in a little hot oil over a high flame.

Only a small amount of oil is used in stir-frying.

Stir-frying is best carried out in a wok. The technique relies on the food being centred over the flame and constantly rotated and turned so that it does not burn.

Vegetables for stir-frying can be blanched in boiling water for a second before stir-frying, if desired.

For better stir-frying result cut vegetables like celery, carrots and beans at an oblique angle. They'll cook faster and absorb more flavour.

Marinate meat or chicken before stir-frying in a mixture of 2 tablespoons soy sauce, 1 dessertspoon cornflour and 1 dessertspoon dry sherry.

MEAT, FISH AND POULTRY

Meat, poultry and fish are major sources of the protein we need in our diet. When buying red meat, look for a good colour (bright red and close-grained flesh in beef, dull red in mutton, pink in lamb, veal and pork). Fat should be firm, and the outside fat should be cream in beef and white in lamb, mutton, veal and pork. All meat should smell fresh. Remember it can be false economy to buy cheap cuts, as they contain more gristle and bone.

Poultry should look smooth and the breast soft and pliable — which you can't always assess if you buy frozen or cling-wrapped poultry at the supermarket. Although supermarket poultry is usually of consistent quality, it doesn't compare in flavour with birds bought at a specialist poultry shop. Here you can choose from a huge range of size and type: boiling fowls, ducks, turkeys and roasting birds — including free-range and corn-fed — smaller spatchcocks and poussins for special occasions, as well as game birds such as quail and pheasant. Corn-fed poultry has a yellow tinge to the flesh. Remember to keep giblets, feet and necks for stock or gravy.

Choose fish that are in season, that is, cheap, plentiful and of good quality. The flesh should be firm and bright and the eyes not sunken — which could indicate that the fish is not fresh.

Beef

When buying beef, remember that older ox beef will have more flavour and is a darker red than younger yearling meat, although the young meat and veal are usually very tender.

The tender cuts of beef with little connective tissue can be roasted, pan fried or grilled; the tough cuts should be cooked by moist heat methods to soften the tissue.

The tenderness of tough cuts can be improved before cooking by grinding, mincing, cubing, pounding or marinating.

Pan fry or grill fillet, rump, porterhouse or T-bone steaks.

Roast fillet or rump (in the piece), wing ring, sirloin or corner cuts of topside, rib roasts and bolar.

Braise larger pieces of topside, bolar and blade steak.

Casserole chopped pieces of topside, skirt and round steak, and gravy beef.

Beef casserole

The secret of successful casserole cooking is the long slow cooking that tenderises the fibres in cheaper cuts of meat.

This tasty beef casserole serves six. Preheat oven to 200°C. In a frying pan, cook 2 chopped rashers bacon and 2 sliced onions in 2 tablespoons olive oil over medium heat. Remove to casserole dish. Chop 1 kg round or blade steak into 2.5 cm cubes and dredge with plain flour. Brown meat cubes in frying pan and add to casserole dish. Add 1 tablespoon flour to frying pan and a little more oil if needed, blend and cook for 2 minutes over low heat. Add 2 dessertspoons tomato paste, 1½ cups red wine and 1 cup water or stock. Bring to simmer, stirring. Pour this over the meat in the casserole and add salt, freshly ground black pepper, 2 bay leaves, 2 chopped stalks celery, 3 chopped peeled carrots and 2 chopped peeled tomatoes. Cover tightly and cook in 200°C oven for 15 minutes, then reduce heat to 150°C for 75 minutes.

This recipe can be varied in lots of ways. Try substituting 1½ cups beer for the red wine. Or if you prefer, substitute a well-flavoured stock.

Another variation is to add
8-10 chopped black olives
with the vegetables (leave
out the salt in the recipe as
the olives are salty).

Or you could sauté 250 g
mushrooms and add
them.

More unusual additions to
a casserole might be sliced
leeks, kernels of sweet corn,
fresh orange peel, a heaped
tablespoon of chutney,
chopped fennel, diced
turnip or whole shallots.

Try rubbing the inside of
your casserole dish with
garlic — this will add to the
flavour without being too
strong for non-garlic
eaters.

Remember, for a tasty
casserole you must brown

the meat thoroughly and
quickly to give it a good
flavour.

Beef — minced
Beef trimmings are minced
and form the basis of many
low-cost easy-to-prepare
beef meals, including
sausages.

The fat in mince is
necessary for flavour and
improves the texture of
meat loaves, meat balls
and similar dishes.

Hamburger mince is
usually a combination of
finely minced beef, lamb,
pork and veal and is best
used for hamburgers, meat
balls, meat loaves, and as
a substitute in recipes
requiring finely minced
beef.

Sausage mince is made of beef and lamb offcuts together with cereal, water and seasonings. It is best used for stuffings, sausage patties and sausage rolls.

Beef — roasting

Always roast beef in a hot oven. This will produce a crisp brown outside and a pink inside to the joint.

Do not overcook it. Check the recommended roasting temperatures in the chapter on tips and techniques.

Traditional accompaniments for roast beef are roast potatoes and Yorkshire pudding, which can be cooked in the pan with the beef if there is room, or in a separate pan.

Here is a simple recipe for Yorkshire pudding. Sift 2 heaped tablespoons plain flour with 1 teaspoon salt. Make a well in the centre and drop in an egg. Gradually add ¾ cup milk, stirring in the flour to make a thick batter. Leave to stand for at least 1 hour. Pour the batter into a roasting pan containing hot dripping and bake for 15-20 minutes in the hot oven.

Allow roast beef to stand for 5-10 minutes with the oven door open after cooking time has finished. This lets the juices set before carving.

Serve roast beef with brown gravy. Pour off most of the fat from the roasting pan, leaving a tablespoon or two. Thicken the fat with 2 tablespoons plain flour and stir over heat until brown. Add 2 cups warm water or stock and stir over low heat until the gravy is thickened. Season with salt and pepper.

Two tablespoons of brandy poured over a beef or veal roast 20 minutes before it goes into the oven will tenderise the meat.

Fish

Fish deteriorates very quickly, so make sure it is fresh when you buy it, and don't keep it in the refrigerator longer than 2 days.

Shellfish should be wrapped in foil or placed in a covered container in the refrigerator and used within 3 days.

Buy your fish according to seasonal availability — it should be plentiful and cheap.

Buying whole fish is more economical than fillets. Use the trimmings and head to make soup or sauces.

Fish does not require long cooking — although it must be cooked right through. It will be dry if overcooked.

Fish is cooked when the flesh is no longer translucent and when it flakes at the touch of a knife.

Wash fish before you refrigerate it and dry with

paper towels. Cover with foil rather than plastic film, which makes fish sweat.

Fish tastes best accompanied by freshly squeezed lemon juice, tartare sauce, chopped capers, watercress, dill, parsley and fennel.

Fish — cooking
Fillets of white-fleshed fish, such as whiting, garfish, snapper, bream, flathead, red fish and flounder, are best lightly fried, grilled or steamed.

Rub the frying pan with salt and warm it slightly then wipe out before frying fish. It won't stick to the pan.

Don't overcrowd the pan when frying fish. The moisture in the flesh will reduce the fat temperature and the fish will 'stew' and disintegrate. Fry only one or two pieces of fish at a time to cook them quickly and have a crisp finish.

Poach or bake larger whole fish that will hold together. First make a stock by boiling 1 sliced onion, 1 bay leaf, a piece of celery, 1 chopped carrot, salt and pepper in 2 cups water for 15 minutes. Strain off the vegetables and poach the fish gently in the liquid. Reduce the liquid further after cooking and spoon over the fish before serving.

Poached fish is delicious served cold with aioli (garlic mayonnaise).

Poaching fish in stock or wine with a slice of onion, a few slices of fresh ginger and a few strands of lemon grass will give it a subtle Asian flavour.

Fish should be frequently basted during grilling or barbecuing — fillets dry out very quickly.

Fish with darker or oilier flesh, such as sardines, tuna, mullet and salmon, can be grilled or baked.

Fish in foil
Use the wrapping method for baking fish to conserve flavour and moisture.

You can use any whole fish of reasonable size — snapper, bream or trout. Fish should weigh at least 500 g for a good result.

Preheat oven to 180°C. Place fish on a sheet of cooking foil and dot with a little butter, chopped herbs (parsley, dill, rosemary), salt and freshly ground black pepper. Pour over ½ cup dry white wine. Wrap the fish and bake for 20-30 minutes or until the flesh is cooked. Carefully peel the skin off the fish and place on a serving dish. Spoon over the strained cooking liquid and garnish with parsley.

You can also wrap fish to be baked in spinach or cabbage leaves.

Fish — steaming
A fish steamer is a good investment. Steaming is a fat-free and nutritious way of preparing food. If you

don't have a steamer, improvise your own by using a wire rack over a large frying pan or frypan of simmering water. You must have a well-fitting lid for satisfactory results.

Take any medium-sized fish — such as snapper or bream — lightly scrape off scales if necessary and place on a plate big enough to hold it. Cover fish with chopped spring onions, chopped peeled fresh ginger, 1 tablespoon soy sauce, 1 tablespoon dry sherry and a little salt and pepper.

Place plate in a steamer or on rack in prepared frypan of simmering water, cover with a lid and steam for 15 minutes or until the eye of

the fish turns white and sticks out. Remove fish on to a serving platter. In a small saucepan, heat 2 tablespoons sesame oil to smoking and pour over the fish just before serving.

Shelled green prawns and scallops are excellent steamed with a little soy sauce and fresh ginger.

Lamb

Lamb is 3-12 months old. The flesh should be fine grained and velvety and a pinkish-red in colour.

Hogget is 1-2 years old. The flesh is medium grained and red in colour.

Mutton is 2 years and over and much the same texture and colour as hogget.

Although not widely available these days, mutton is very tasty and somewhat firmer than lamb.

Choose lamb cuts which can be easily trimmed of fat if you want to cut down on fats. Leg of lamb is the best choice for low-fat cooking.

Grill or pan fry mid loin chops, cutlets, forequarter chops.

Roast leg, loin, crown roast, racks of lamb, whole forequarter, shoulder, saddle and best end of neck.

Casserole forequarter or chump — whole or chops — shoulder neck, breast, shank, cubed leg or shoulder.

When buying lamb, select freshly prepared lean cuts with good colour and moist surfaces. Remove the store wrapping and keep in the refrigerator at the top or in the meat keeper. Cover tightly to prevent surface dryness.

Use within 2-3 days or freeze for later use. Minced lamb should be used within 24 hours of purchase or frozen.

Corned or pumped legs should be refrigerated in their original wrappings and will keep for 5-7 days.

Lamb curry

Use cubed lamb shoulder or leg for an easy curry.

You'll need a heavy heat-proof casserole and 1 kg

lamb shoulder or leg in 2.5 cm cubes to serve four. First soften a sliced onion in a little oil. Dredge meat with flour and toss in oil in the casserole to brown. Add onion, a handful of sultanas, 1 cup water or stock, 1 cup coconut milk, 1 grated apple, 2 tablespoons curry powder or paste, a bay leaf and salt to taste. Simmer on low heat for 1-1½ hours. Add more curry powder if you wish.

Heat curry powder briefly in a frying pan to dry roast it before using. It brings out the flavour. Watch you don't burn it.

Lamb — roasting

Traditionally, roast lamb is served with roast potatoes and other roast vegetables, gravy, mint sauce and/or red currant jelly.

The younger and more tender cuts of lamb can be roasted quickly like beef, and some people prefer lamb to be pink on the inside.

Older meat and larger joints such as forequarter are better roasted for longer periods.

Cut little pockets into the flesh on a leg of lamb and insert slivers of garlic, mint leaves or sprigs of rosemary in each before roasting.

Dip your lamb cutlets in beaten egg and coat with breadcrumbs, then bake in a preheated over on 220°C for 20-30 minutes.

This will give a crisp outside and a pink inside. It is a healthier method than frying.

The flavour of lamb cutlets is enhanced if you marinate them for an hour in a mixture of a little oil, chopped fresh thyme, rosemary, tarragon and freshly ground black pepper before grilling.

Lamb with oregano

This is really roast lamb Greek-style. Oregano is a common herb in Greece; use the dried version if you can't get fresh, but it won't taste the same.

Ask your butcher to take the bone out of a medium-sized leg of lamb. Preheat

the oven to 220°C. Spread the meat out and stuff it with a mixture of a cup of fresh white breadcrumbs, the grated rind and juice of a lemon, 2 crushed cloves garlic, 2 tablespoons chopped fresh oregano or 2 teaspoons dried oregano, salt, freshly ground pepper and a beaten egg to bind it. Fold the meat together over the stuffing and tie with string. Make a paste of 2 tablespoons plain flour, 1 dessertspoon sugar, a pinch paprika, 1 tablespoon fresh chopped oregano or 1 teaspoon dried oregano, freshly ground black pepper and enough olive oil to moisten, and cover the meat with it. Roast for 20 minutes then turn oven down to 180°C for 20 minutes for pink lamb, 30 minutes for well done.

Meat

As a general rule, meat from very young animals will have less flavour than that from older beasts. It will be tender, but may need extra sauces or stuffings.

Young lamb, beef, veal or pork is also a lighter pink colour.

Meat from older animals will have more internal fat, or 'marbling'. During the cooking, this inner fat melts and tenderises the muscular flesh.

The well-marbled cuts of meat are the most expensive as they are the most tender.

Less fat is found on the parts of the beast that are most exercised — like the hind legs. These cuts will not be as tender, but can be very tasty when given long, slow cooking, as in a casserole. Examples of cheaper cuts are round, blade and chuck steak, chump chops, brisket and necks.

Expensive cuts include fillet and rump steak, wing rib roast, middle loin lamb chops, legs of lamb, pork loin or leg. These need minimum preparation and can be cooked by simply grilling or roasting.

Meat — cooking

Never cook meat immediately after taking it out of

the refrigerator. Always allow it to reach room temperature or it will be tough.

Do not salt meat when you are exposing it to direct heat. Salt will toughen the fibres. Sprinkle on other seasonings but keep the salt until after cooking.

If you add too much salt to stews or casseroles simply toss in some raw peeled potato. The potato will absorb the salt. Discard before serving.

Meat — leftovers
Always cover leftover meats with cling film and refrigerate — they can be kept for 2 or 3 days.

To use up leftover meat, try a cassoulet dish. Soak

250 g haricot beans overnight in an ovenproof casserole, then cook the beans and liquid over a low flame with a chopped onion and salt and pepper for about an hour. Add a crushed clove of garlic, 2 rashers chopped bacon, the chopped leftover meat, some sliced cooked sausage and a couple of chopped tomatoes. Season to taste and simmer for another hour. Add a little wine if desired.

Offal
All offal should be used as soon as you buy it. It deteriorates very quickly. Frozen offal will keep safely for one month.

Soak brains in salted water and remove the outer

membranes. Brains may be fried in a coating of egg and breadcrumbs in a little butter, or poached lightly in simmering water and then served in a white sauce.

Small sheep's kidneys are easy to prepare. Remove the membrane, slice in two and fry in a little butter or bacon fat. Add a dash of worcestershire sauce and salt and pepper for a devilled finish. Serve with bacon.

Lamb's liver, or lamb's fry, is a dish that's easy to prepare, but the secret is in the fast cooking and in slicing the liver wafer-thin. Carefully remove the membrane and any coarse tubes and slice the liver

horizontally as thinly as you can. Lightly dredge with plain flour and fry for 20 seconds each side in a little butter. Add a little dry sherry to the pan juices, blend and serve immediately with crisp bacon or mashed potato.

Soak fresh tongues for 1 hour in lightly salted water with a dash of vinegar. Rinse. To cook, cover tongue with cold water in a good-sized pan and season with onion, peppercorns, cloves or parsley. Bring slowly to the boil, reduce heat, cover and simmer. The meat will offer no resistance when pierced with a skewer when it is done. Peel off the thick outer skin and remove any bone and gristle. Serve sliced, with mustard or caper sauce.

Blanching will improve tripe before you cook it. Simmer blanched tripe with milk, water, onion, vegetables and seasonings until tender (about 1½ hours), then thicken the cooking liquid before serving. Plain cooked tripe can be drained, cooled and dipped in flour, egg and breadcrumbs then deep fried.

Oxtail

Oxtail can be made into a gourmet casserole. Preheat oven to 200°C. Fry a couple of chopped rashers of bacon in a little oil and remove to a heavy casserole. Dredge the oxtail portions in a little flour,

brown them in the fat and remove to the casserole. Fry a couple of onions in the fat and add to casserole. Add a little more oil to the pan with 1 heaped tablespoon of flour, mix to a paste, cook for a minute and then add 2 cups water or stock to the roux. Stir to a gravy, season well with salt and freshly ground black pepper. Add this to the casserole along with 1 cup of red wine, 1 peeled chopped carrot, 1 chopped stalk of celery, 1 bay leaf and 1 crushed clove of garlic. Bring to a simmer in the oven, then reduce heat to 150°C or a slow simmer and cook for 2-3 hours or until the meat comes away from the bones. Add more liquid if necessary.

Pork

Pork is one of the oldest foods known and one of the tastiest and best loved. Pork is a tender meat as pigs don't exercise like cattle and sheep. This means most cuts of pork can be grilled or pan fried.

Pork requires thorough cooking to kill bacteria and develop its flavours, although the golden rule is never to cook pork too quickly or for too long. Pink-coloured pork should never be eaten.

Roast the leg, loin, fillet, shoulder or neck and spareribs.

Grill or pan fry loin chops, steaks, butterfly steaks, fillet and spareribs.

Casserole or braise chops, diced leg or shoulder, or neck.

Boil pickled pork or pumped leg of pork.

Stir-fry fillet or medallions.

Pork fillet is a good substitute for veal in recipes requiring escalopes. It can be sliced thinly and beaten flat, then pan-fried.

When buying pork, choose lean meat that is pale pink, without gristle and firm to touch. It should be slightly marbled and have milky white fat.

Pork fillet with ginger

Use as many pork fillets as you need — a fillet will

usually serve two people. Prepare a marinade of ½ cup beef, chicken or vegetable stock, ¼ cup soy sauce, ⅓ cup honey, 1 teaspoon salt and 1 dessertspoon chopped fresh ginger or 1 teaspoon dried ground ginger. Soak fillets in this mixture for at least 2 hours. Preheat oven to 180°C. Remove fillets from the marinade and roast for 30-40 minutes. Bring the marinade to a simmer on the stove and reduce slightly.

Serve the marinade with the sliced fillets as a sauce.

Pork — roast

On a traditional pork roast with rind, the butcher will score the skin or rind finely to make a crackling.

The secret of crisp brown crackling is to rub the rind with oil and salt. Cook in a moderately hot oven (160-200°C).

Check suggested cooking times in the chapter on tips and techniques.

Roast pork should be served with an apple sauce and brown gravy.

A stuffing of 1 chopped onion, 1 cup fresh white breadcrumbs, a handful of chopped raisins and salt and pepper will make the roast tasty. Pork tends to be a bland meat.

If you roast pork without the rind, use an oven bag or

roast in a moderate oven to reduce shrinkage.

Like beef, pork should be allowed to stand for 10 minutes before carving to allow the juices to set.

Poultry
Poultry is very susceptible to bacterial growth. Never refreeze poultry once it has already been frozen.

Use defrosted poultry immediately after it thaws.

Make sure poultry is completely defrosted before you cook it to avoid any risk of it remaining un-cooked and perhaps con-taminated in the middle.

You should cook fresh chicken within 2-3 days of purchase.

Use whole chickens to roast or steam.

Two smaller chickens (with their two extra legs) feed more people than one larger bird.

Split spatchcocks along the backbone for a different way of serving. Flatten them out in a roasting pan. Preheat oven to 200°C. Dot the breast and thighs with butter and chopped fresh tarragon, and pour over a cup of chicken stock, salt, pepper and the juice of $1/2$ lemon. Roast the birds for 1 hour, basting frequently. Add more stock if it seems necessary and cover with foil if the breast becomes too brown. Serve with the pan juices as a sauce.

Poached or boiled chicken

Use a good-sized bird to poach or boil. Put the chicken in a large pan. Add water to almost cover it. Bring to the boil, skim the surface and add 1 sliced onion, piece of carrot and celery, slice of lemon and salt and pepper. Turn down the heat until the liquid is barely simmering and cook for 1 hour or until flesh is tender.

Boiled fowl can be served with egg, caper or parsley sauce.

Use the meat from a boiled fowl to prepare dishes such as Chicken à la King (in white sauce), chicken in aspic, or use cold in salads.

Pot-cooked chicken pieces

Use chicken pieces in a wide variety of ways. Dredge them with flour, brown in oil and butter, then cook in apricot nectar or cider. Add a little cream to make a sauce.

Here's a simple but delicious chicken dish using chicken pieces. Dredge 1 kg skinned chicken pieces with plain flour and brown in 1 tablespoon butter mixed with 1 tablespoon olive oil. Pour over 1 tablespoon brandy and flame. Remove chicken pieces and any liquid to a casserole dish that can be used on the stove top. Wipe the frying pan. Soften 250 g sliced button mushrooms and

1 small chopped white onion in 1 tablespoon butter, add ½ cup chicken stock or water, ½ cup dry white wine, 1 tablespoon chopped fresh tarragon or 1 teaspoon dry tarragon, 2 dessertspoons tomato paste, salt and freshly ground black pepper. Bring this to a simmer, pour over the chicken pieces in the casserole, cover tightly and cook for 45 minutes over a low flame. Stir once or twice during cooking.

Roast chicken

Roast chicken is traditionally stuffed with fresh breadcrumbs and herbs, bound with a beaten egg or with sausage meat. Stand the chicken on a rack in the pan and smear the breast with dripping or butter and a little oil. Fix several rashers of bacon across the breast and roast in a 200°C oven for 1-1½ hours for the average bird. Baste frequently with fat and pan juices. Serve with brown gravy, bread sauce and roast potatoes.

Don't let poultry dry out when roasting. Cover the breast with foil or greased brown paper.

Boost the flavour of roast chicken by inserting an apple studded with cloves and garlic into the cavity before roasting.

To make a roast chicken deliciously golden, brush it with milk, dust it with plain flour and baste it with melted butter before roasting.

To make bread sauce, simply peel an onion and stud it with cloves. Simmer it with 6 whole peppercorns in 1¼ cups milk for 15 minutes. Strain, and pour the seasoned liquid over ½ cup fresh white breadcrumbs. Season with a pinch of cayenne pepper and salt, and add 1 tablespoon cream. Reheat the sauce gently.

Roast duck

Ducks are very fatty. Use this method of roasting to get rid of excess fat.

Prick the bird all over and roast at 240°C for 20 minutes, remove from pan and pour off the accumulated fat. Then return to pan, butter the breast and season with salt and pepper. Finish the roasting at 200°C for 40-60 minutes. This method will guarantee a crisp skin and moist but non-greasy meat.

Roast duck is served stuffed with a sage, onion and fresh breadcrumb mixture bound with a beaten egg, and roast potatoes and apple sauce.

Most game birds — such as pheasant, squab and quail — are now available as domesticated fowls. Their flesh is slightly darker than that of chicken, but not as strong as that of wild game.

Be careful not to let the flesh of game birds dry out in cooking. An oven bag will conserve the juices and ensure a moist finish.

Veal

Milk-fed veal comes from very young calves. It is usually expensive and has little fat. Veal which comes from older animals is a deeper colour.

Baby veal is a white fine meat that needs very little cooking. The shoulder or leg meat of the milk-fed calf is sold for escalopes. Simply dredge with flour, toss in butter and a little lemon and white wine for a quick, delicious meal.

To keep escalopes flat in the frying pan, make a few

small cuts around the edges with a sharp knife.

Veal has a less pronounced flavour than red meat and therefore goes well with a tasty gravy or sauce as an accompaniment.

Roast the leg, loin, shoulder and breast of veal.

Grill or pan fry loin chops and steak taken from the rump or even the leg. Veal chops with the kidneys are taken from the loin.

Veal cutlets will stay tender if you pan fry them slowly until nearly cooked then finish the cooking at a reduced temperature in a little milk.

Casserole cubed meat from the neck and breast.

Veal shanks are used to make osso bucco.

Traditional schnitzel and escalope slices are usually taken from the leg.

Minced veal is made from carcass trimmings, although these are usually mixed with pork trimmings for veal and pork mince.

For pure veal mince, use shoulder or cubed veal and either ask the butcher to mince it for you or do it yourself at home.

Veal parcels
This dish is simple but rich. To serve eight, take 8 thin slices of veal. Lay them out and on each place 1 slice of ham, 1 dessertspoon parmesan cheese, a pinch cayenne pepper and 1 heaped tablespoon button mushrooms, softened in a little butter. Roll up the veal slices into tight parcels and tie them with string. Melt 2 tablespoons butter in a heavy pan and brown the parcels all over. Pour over 1 tablespoon brandy, $1/2$ cup chicken stock and $1/2$ cup pure cream. Cover the pan and cook slowly for 15-20 minutes, basting the parcels occasionally with the liquid.

Veal - smoked
Topside of silverside from medium or heavy veal is cured, smoked and cooked. It is a lean meat with a delicate smoky flavour and is an excellent substitute for ham.

DAIRY PRODUCTS

Milk, butter and cheese are very valuable sources of protein, fat, vitamins, calcium and other minerals in our diet. These foods can be eaten as they are, or used as basic ingredients in many delicious sauces, cakes, desserts and savoury dishes. Composed of simple fats, butter is unmatched for its flavour-enhancing and preserving qualities and is easily digestible. Cream adds body and richness that transforms an ordinary dish into something special. Cheese is rich in protein and is a good alternative food to meat. For those on low-fat diets, there are now reduced-fat cheeses, milk and yoghurt which are palatable alternatives to standard produce.

Dairy produce is extremely perishable and should be stored in the refrigerator. Note carefully the use-by dates on milk, cream, yoghurt, butter and cheese.

In this chapter, there are suggestions on how to make milk puddings, custards and cheese dishes both sweet and savoury.

Butter

Keep butter covered both in the cupboard or pantry and in the refrigerator. It tends to absorb the odours from other foods.

Butter is more easily digested than other fats because of its low melting point and high content of simple fats.

Light also spoils the flavour of butter.

When melting butter for a recipe, heat it gently. If it gets too hot it will make the finished product taste greasy.

Keep butter refrigerated until you are ready to use it.

Unsalted butter is more perishable than salted butter.

Clarified butter, or ghee, has a higher burning point than butter. Use it for pan frying and sautéeing.

To make garlic butter, blanch 4 peeled cloves of garlic in boiling water for 5 minutes then drain. Crush the garlic and beat it into 60 g creamed butter with pepper. Use on red meats and prawns, or for garlic bread.

To make lemon butter, beat the grated rind of a lemon and a teaspoon of lemon juice in 60 g creamed butter. Use on fish and vegetables.

When using butter in pan frying add a dessertspoon of any oil (except olive). This stops the butter burning.

Cheese

Cheese is made from fermented milk. A basic rule of thumb is the softer the cheese, the shorter the keeping time.

As a general rule, hard cheese has a higher percentage of protein to fat. Soft cheese has more fat and less protein.

Use cottage cheese in salads, with fruit in sandwiches and dips and in cheesecakes. Ricotta is good in omelettes and desserts or you can bake it and then drizzle it with olive oil.

Store all cheese, except the very hard varieties such as parmesan, in the refrigerator.

Wrapping firm cheeses in foil before refrigerating will keep them fresh.

Always allow cheese to reach room temperature and develop its flavour before using it in cooking, or you won't be able to judge the correct quantity to use in a recipe.

Sharp cheddar cheese is perfect with a tart Granny Smith apple. Corella pears and slivers of parmesan are also delicious.

Cheese should be cooked over a gentle heat or it will go tough and stringy.

Leave baked cheesecakes to cool in the oven with the door open after baking time is finished. They won't shrink or crack.

Rub the cut edge of cheese with butter or margarine to stop it going hard.

Cheese grated on a wet plate will slide off more easily.

Keep grated cheese in a screw-topped jar in the refrigerator. A sugar cube in the jar will keep it from going mouldy.

Cheese and ham sandwich special

Liberally butter 2 slices of white bread. Spread a little French mustard on the other side of one slice and lie a slice of ham and a slice of Swiss or gruyère cheese on top. Sandwich the 2 halves together and fry on the buttered outsides till golden brown and the cheese has melted in the middle of the sandwich.

Cream

Liquid cream can make dishes bland, so always test for flavour as you add it.

If cream has been over-beaten, slowly fold in a dessertspoon of very cold milk.

A teaspoon of vanilla added while beating will help keep cream firm.

To sweeten whipped cream, use icing sugar and add it at the end of the whipping.

If thin cream won't whip, try adding an ice cube as a thickener.

Another trick is to stand the bowl in cold water while beating.

Or you can add an egg
white — but don't use this
cream for any keeping
purpose. Use it to serve
immediately.

As a last resort, gradually
whip in three or four drops
of lemon juice.

Crêpes

Crêpes can be a delicious
dessert if sprinkled with
caster sugar and lemon and
served with ice cream, or
stuffed with fruit purée or
jam.

For savoury crêpes to serve
as a light meal or entrée,
stuff the crêpes with a
mixture of cooked chicken
and mushrooms in white
sauce, ham and Swiss
cheese, chopped ham and
button mushrooms in white

sauce, or puréed spinach,
pine nuts and raisins. Top
the crêpes with a little
cheese before reheating.

Crêpes — basic batter

Sift 2 tablespoons plain
flour into a bowl with 1
teaspoon salt, make a well
in the middle and put in 1
egg and 1 teaspoon olive
oil. Blend, then gradually
add 1 cup milk and mix to
a thin, smooth batter.
Allow to rest for at least 1
hour.

Add a stiffly beaten egg
white to the rested batter
for extra light crepes.

To cook crêpes, heat 1/2
teaspoon butter in a small
pan with a heavy base.
When the butter is foaming

but not too brown, add enough batter to barely cover the bottom. Shake the pan as the mixture cooks to keep it from sticking. When bubbles appear on the surface of the crêpe, flip it over to the other side and finish cooking. As you finish, stack the crêpes up with greaseproof paper between them and leave in a warm place until you are ready to use them.

Custard
Custards are mixtures of milk, eggs and sugar (for sweet custards).

You can flavour sweet custards with vanilla or almond essence or by infusing a bay leaf in the milk for a few minutes.

Always cook custards slowly or they will curdle.

Prevent a skin forming on custards by sprinkling a small amount of sugar over the top.

If you want your custard to set, allow 4 eggs to every 2 cups milk.

A baked custard should be cooked standing in a dish of water in the oven to protect it from direct heat.

For a custard that is to be turned out, grease the pie dish to enable the custard to slide out easily. Remove custard from the heat immediately it is set to avoid curdling.

Custard cooked on the stove top is best stirred in a

double saucepan away from the direct heat.

If you are using a normal saucepan, it must have a heavy base and you must stir the mixture constantly over a low heat.

Mock custards can be made with cornflour or a commercial custard powder.

Custard — baked caramel

Preheat oven to 150°C. Put a metal pie dish in the oven to warm. Heat 2 tablespoons sugar with 1 tablespoon water and 1 tablespoon lemon juice in a saucepan until the sugar is dissolved, then boil till brown in colour. Pour the caramel into the warm pie dish and tip it around so

the bottom and sides are coated. Beat up 4 large eggs and add 2 good cups warm milk, a pinch of salt and 2 tablespoons sugar while beating. Pour the mixture into the pie dish, set this in a dish of water and bake in the oven for 30-40 minutes or until set.

To test a baked custard for doneness, insert a flat knife into the centre. The blade should come out clean.

Custard — stove top

Beat together 2 egg yolks and 1 whole egg with 1 tablespoon sugar and a few drops of vanilla essence. Add 2 cups warm milk while still beating. Pour into the top of a double saucepan and stir over a low heat with a wooden spoon until the custard thickens and coats the spoon. Don't let the water in the base of the double saucepan get too hot.

If you use an ordinary saucepan to cook this custard, you must take great care not to let the mixture get too hot or it will curdle.

You can improvise a double saucepan by standing the mixture in a heatproof glass jug in a saucepan of hot water.

If the custard curdles, remove it from the heat, stand it in cold water in the sink and try beating vigorously. If this doesn't

work, mix a little cornflour with cold water and mix it into the custard. Return it to the heat and stir just long enough to cook the flour and thicken the custard.

Egg flip

To make an egg flip for one, place in a blender 2 cups cold milk, ½ teaspoon vanilla essence, 1 dessert-spoon sugar and 1 egg. Blend well and top with a pinch of nutmeg to serve.

For a variation, use other flavourings instead of the vanilla — a little blended instant coffee or chocolate powder.

To make an egg milkshake, leave out the sugar and vanilla and add 1 or 2

tablespoons vanilla ice
cream.

Ice cream

Ice cream can be made with
cream, rich milk, custard or
evaporated milk and sweetened and flavoured with
nuts, glacé fruits, fruit
purées or liqueurs.

Don't add too much sugar
to ice cream mixes, as sugar
will prevent freezing.

An hour after you have put
the mixture in the freezer,
take it out and beat it again
and then refreeze.

This will ensure a smooth
cream.

Make your flavouring
strong, as freezing will
dissipate it.

However, too much alcohol
in the mixture will stop the
ice cream freezing well.

Milk

Absolute cleanliness is
required when handling
milk, as it is the perfect
medium for the growth of
bacteria.

Pasteurised milk will keep
as long as two weeks in the
refrigerator.

Milk easily picks up odours
and flavours from other
foods, so keep milk cool,
clean and covered — in the
refrigerator.

Light will destroy the
vitamins in milk.

Milk boils over very easily.
To prevent this, stand a
spoon in the saucepan.

Rinse your milk saucepan in cold water before boiling milk; it will not stick to the sides.

If you are freezing milk, let it defrost in the refrigerator to avoid contamination at room temperature.

Milk puddings

Milk puddings are usually made from bread or rice, milk and sugar. Sometimes eggs are added.

To stop a skin forming on cooked milk puddings, sprinkle them with sugar.

Milk puddings should not be dry. Do not cook them quickly.

If you are cooking milk puddings on the top of the stove, don't use a thin saucepan; choose one with a heavy base to avoid the milk catching.

Make sure you stir milk puddings well so that they cook evenly throughout.

Add a pinch of salt to all milk puddings to enhance the flavour.

No-fail cheesecake

Crush 2 cups semi-sweet biscuits and add 3 tablespoons melted butter to bind them together. Press into a greased 20-cm springform pan. Beat 2 cups cream cheese until soft and add a tin of sweetened condensed milk and 1/2 cup lemon juice. Pour this into the crumb case and refrigerate for 3 hours.

Unmould to serve. Decorate with seasonal fruit.

Orange butter

Crêpes can be stuffed with an orange butter to make the classic crêpes suzette. Cream together 2 tablespoons butter and 2 tablespoons caster sugar until soft.

Gradually add 2 teaspoons orange rind, 1 teaspoon lemon juice, 1 tablespoon Kirsch or Curaçao and 1 dessertspoon grated orange rind.

Put a little of the filling on each crêpe, roll up and sprinkle with icing sugar. Just before serving, pour over a little rum or brandy and ignite.

Quiche lorraine

Take a quantity of shortcrust pastry (*see* chapter on cakes and pastry), roll out and line a greased springform tin (18-20 cm). Preheat oven to 200°C. In a bowl beat 2 eggs with 1¼ cups cream. Add ¼ cup diced Swiss cheese, ¼ cup chopped bacon, salt (only a little — the bacon is salty) and freshly ground black pepper. Pour the mixture into the dough case and sprinkle with chopped parsley. Bake for about 30 minutes or until the custard is set and golden brown.

Beat the filling mixtures for your quiches with a balloon whisk to make them light.

If the oven is too hot, quiche fillings will curdle.

Raspberry ice cream

Fold 1 cup raspberry purée (*see* chapter on vegetables and fruit), into 2 cups beaten pure cream. Add a little lemon juice and sugar if needed, and spoon into an ice-cream tray.

Freeze, take out after 1 hour and beat, then refreeze. Remove ice cream to normal refrigerator section for 30 minutes before serving.

Vary this recipe by adding slightly sweetened mango or passionfruit pulp instead of raspberry.

Other variations: melted chocolate or instant coffee dissolved in evaporated milk, or dried fruit soaked in liqueur.

Rice pudding

The secret of rice pudding is long cooking and the absorbing of the milk into the rice to make a creamy consistency. Don't let the pudding dry out.

Long grain rice is no good for a rice pudding. The grains won't absorb the milk to give a creamy result.

Turn the oven on to low. Put 4 tablespoons white rice in a greased ovenproof dish with ½ cup boiling water and leave to stand in the warm oven until the rice has absorbed the water. Pour in 3 cups milk and leave to stand for another 10 minutes.

Add 1 tablespoon sultanas, grated rind of 1 lemon, 1 dessertspoon butter and 3 tablespoons sugar.

Stand in a dish of warm water, turn the oven up to 125°C and cook for about 2 hours, stirring occasionally.

Add another cup of milk after 1 hour.

Scotsman's delight

Pure cream can be used to make simple rich desserts by folding in flavourings such as coffee, chocolate or fruit liqueur.

Beat 2 cups pure cream until stiff, fold in 5 tablespoons honey and 6 tablespoons Scotch whisky. Serve in small glasses.

Vanilla ice cream

Beat 4 eggs until thick, adding ¼ cup caster sugar while beating. Fold in 1 cup beaten cream. In a separate bowl beat ¾ cup cold evaporated milk with 1 teaspoon vanilla until it is thick. Fold this into the cream and yolk mixture. then in another bowl beat 4 egg whites and ¼ cup caster sugar until stiff. Fold into the mixture and freeze until set.

Yoghurt

Use yoghurt as a substitute for cream in low-fat diets.

If a recipe requires yoghurt or sour cream, and you have none, add a dessert-spoon of lemon and a pinch of salt to ordinary cream.

Fold fruit purées or flavourings into plain or vanilla yoghurt and freeze in small containers. If you insert icy pole sticks they are a treat for children.

EGGS

Eggs are a good source of both protein and vitamins and are a staple item in our diet. You can build a meal around an egg by simply boiling or poaching it, or by combining it with other ingredients to make more elaborate soufflés, omelettes, pies or salads. Eggs are used to thicken and enrich sauces and soups, as raising agents in cakes and puddings, to bind stuffing ingredients and to glaze foods to enhance their appearance.

Eggs come in their own natural wrapping, which will keep them fresh in the refrigerator for months, or in a cool place for weeks. If purchased from reputable suppliers, their quality is guaranteed. Always note the size of the eggs you are buying. Unless otherwise stipulated, when recipes ask for eggs use medium-sized ones (about 55 g). Very large or very small eggs may cause an imbalance in ingredients. Remember that two duck eggs are equal to three hen eggs.

In this chapter, there are a number of tips on the best ways to use eggs in simple recipes. Always take them out of the refrigerator at least an hour before using, otherwise the yolks tend to dry out when the shells are broken.

Beating eggs

Always have a grease-free, perfectly dry bowl to beat egg whites. Plastic bowls harbour grease, so use metal, china or glass.

Although an electric beater is acceptable, you should have a copper bowl and wire whisk to beat egg whites. The action of the whisk against the copper oxidises the albumen in the whites and helps them to stay stiff when beaten. Do not wash the bowl in detergent; wipe it out with salt and vinegar or lemon juice.

Slightly stale egg whites will beat better than fresh ones and retain their volume longer.

Egg whites won't beat if there is any yolk in the mixture. Remove any bits of yolk with a piece of the egg shell; the yolk will cling to it.

You can also remove any bits of shell from the bowl this way.

Eggs for beating should be at room temperature. They take about an hour to reach room temperature after refrigeration.

If you heat the beater or bowl before use, egg whites will beat up faster.

Add a pinch of salt or cream of tartar to egg whites before beating to make them extra stiff. Don't use salt if you're making a soufflé though;

it tends to make the whites foamy.

Beaten egg yolks often stick to the sides of the bowl so before adding yolks rinse out your bowl with cold water, throw out the excess water than add the yolks. They will slide out easily after beating.

When you are beating more than one egg together, break the eggs one at a time into a cup to avoid spoiling the whole mixture if one is stale.

Boiled eggs

To boil an egg, either lower a room-temperature egg gently into boiling water and boil for 3½-4 minutes, or put the egg into cold water, bring it to the boil and boil for 2½-3 minutes.

A third method is to bring a saucepan of water to the boil, lower the egg into the water and turn off the heat. Leave the egg in the water for 6 minutes.

Add a little vinegar to the water if the egg shell cracks when you are boiling it. This will stop the egg white pouring out of the shell.

Always pierce the blunt end of an egg with a sharp needle before you lower it into boiling water to stop it cracking. (The air bubble in the blunt end of an egg expands when heated and this causes the cracking.)

Hard-boiled eggs will peel easily and quickly if they

are run under cold water and tapped gently at each end.

Curdling

To rescue a sauce or custard containing eggs that starts to curdle, add a teaspoon or two of cold water and beat vigorously.

Custards cooked on the stove top won't curdle if you add 1 teaspoon cornflour for every 2 cups of milk and egg mixture.

Eggs are coagulated by heat, so it is better to cook them slowly at low temperatures.

When adding egg yolks to a hot sauce, whip a little of the sauce into the eggs, a dessertspoon at a time, until the mixture can safely be returned to the rest of the hot sauce. Don't let the mixture get too hot after the yolks have been added or it will curdle.

Egg and bacon pie

Egg and bacon pie is simple to make and is a great picnic or lunch dish. Preheat oven to 180°C. Grease a deep pie pan. For a pie to feed six people, take at least 250 g of puff pastry (*see* the chapter on cakes and pastry for the puff pastry recipe), and roll it out. Line the bottom and sides of the pan leaving enough pastry to cover the pie and decorate the top. Trim the rinds off 8 rashers bacon, cut into 5-cm lengths and lie half on the pastry. Break 8 eggs into the pan, add freshly ground black pepper to taste and a little salt. Sprinkle with chopped parsley. Lie the rest of the bacon on top, then cover with the rest of the pastry. Crimp edges and decorate the top. Glaze the top with a little beaten egg and milk and bake 20-30 minutes or until golden and the eggs are risen and cooked.

Egg and bacon pie can also be made with shortcrust pastry. *See* the chapter on cakes and pastry for recipe.

French toast
To make French toast for four, lightly beat 4 eggs with 1 tablespoon milk. Separately dip 4 slices of bread in the mixture,

making sure to coat both sides. Drain off excess liquid.

Heat sufficient butter or margarine to cover the bottom of a frying pan. Fry the bread slices until golden on each side. Serve with caster sugar and lemon juice, honey, jam or golden syrup.

Fried eggs
Heat a little butter or lard in a pan until it is bubbling. Break the egg into a cup and slide it into the pan to avoid breaking.

Keep the pan at moderate heat or the whites will toughen.

Never fry too many eggs at once in the pan. They will

be hard to manoeuvre and you will break them.

Fried eggs won't stick to the pan if you sprinkle a little flour over the fat before adding the eggs.

Hard-boiled eggs

Always run cold water over hard-boiled eggs immediately after they are cooked. This will make the shell slip off easily and will stop a black ring forming around the yolks of hard-boiled eggs. Crack the shell at either end, not in the middle.

To cut hard-boiled eggs neatly, use a knife that has been rinsed in hot water.

To make delicious stuffed eggs, cut hard-boiled eggs in half lengthwise and remove the yolks. Mash them with a little mayonnaise, salt, freshly ground black pepper and a handful of chopped herbs: chives, basil, sage, parsley or dill. Replace the yolk mixture inside the white shells and decorate with parsley.

Meringues

Here's a simple meringue recipe. Preheat oven to 220°C. Beat 4 egg whites and a pinch of salt until stiff, but not too dry. Gradually add 1 generous cup caster sugar and lastly a few drops vanilla essence. Turn oven down as low as it will go. Place dessert-spoons of the mixture on oven trays covered with greased paper or foil and cook for at least 4 hours in the warm oven.

Always cook pies with meringue topping slowly to avoid cracking. And when the cooking is finished, leave the pie in the oven with the door open while it cools.

Omelettes
Beat 2 eggs with a little salt and pepper and 1 dessert-spoon cold water. Stir in 1 dessertspoon butter in small pieces. Heat 1 tea-spoon butter in a pan till melted and tip in the mix-ture. Shake pan briskly during cooking and lift the edges of the mixture so that it cooks evenly. When cooked the mixture should be barely set and golden brown underneath.

Fold the omelette over to serve.

If you want to fill your omelette with cheese, bacon, chopped cooked chicken, sautéed vegetables or mushrooms, be sure and have them ready before you start cooking the eggs.

Don't add milk to an omelette mixture; it will make it rubbery and tough. The cold water in the mixture is the secret of a tender omelette — it stops the egg yolks hardening.

Don't use your omelette pan for anything else. Keep it well wiped out with paper towels; don't wash it in water. Salt will remove any scraps that may adhere to it.

An omelette pan should be well seasoned; that is, prepared before use by cooking a little oil in the pan then letting it stand for an hour or so. Wipe out with paper towels.

Don't try to make omelettes too big. Better to cook two small omelettes than one big one when you are serving a number of people. A large omelette tends to burn on the outside without being cooked through.

Another secret of cooking good omelettes is to keep the mixture moving in the pan while you are cooking. This causes the butter to be absorbed into the mixture.

You'll have a greasy omelette if you have too much butter in the pan, or if the butter in the mixture is not absorbed during cooking.

Fold your omelette over before the eggs are set on top — otherwise it will crack.

Don't use margarine to cook omelettes — it contains too much water.

If a fluffy omelette is required, beat the whites of the eggs separately from the yolks and fold them in to the mixture.

When cooking a fluffy or soufflé-type omelette you do not shake the pan or move the mixture while cooking. Just cook gently over a low heat until the underside is golden brown, then place the pan under the griller for a moment to set the top.

Pavlova

Homemade pavlova is delicious filled with whipped cream and topped with strawberries or passionfruit.

A perfect pavlova is simple to make but you must have a really hot oven to start. Preheat oven to 210°C for 20 minutes.

Beat 6 egg whites stiffly, then gradually add 1 cup sugar while still beating. Then fold in 1 dessertspoon white vinegar, 1 tablespoon cornflour and 1 teaspoon vanilla essence. Turn a 20-cm round cake tin upside down, cover with greased paper and pile the mixture in the centre. Place in oven and turn it right down to 100°C. Cook for 1 hour. The mixture will flatten out slightly towards the edges of the cake tin during cooking.

Allow the pavlova to cool in the oven with the door open.

Poached eggs

Bring a pan of water to the boil, add a pinch of salt and a few drops of vinegar. Break an egg into a cup, and slide it into the water. Lower the heat immediately. The vinegar will stop the egg white spreading by coagulating it; it will also keep it a good white colour.

Try poaching eggs in clear stock (chicken or vegetable) for extra flavour.

Scrambled eggs

To make scrambled eggs for one, beat 2 eggs lightly with 1 tablespoon milk, salt and pepper. Barely melt a dessertspoon butter in a small heavy saucepan and stir the egg mixture over a low heat until it begins to set.

To achieve a creamy texture, scrambled eggs must be cooked over a low heat. Add an extra yolk to the mixture before the finish of cooking for extra creaminess.

Do not overcook scrambled eggs. They should not be set firmly when you

remove them from the heat.

If they are overcooked; scrambled eggs will be rubbery and watery.

Vary your scrambled eggs by adding a teaspoon of curry powder, a handful of chives or a chopped peeled tomato.

Don't use milk in the mixture if you are adding tomato — the acid in the tomato will curdle the milk.

Luxurious additions to scrambled eggs, making them into a lunch or entrée dish, include caviar, slivers of smoked salmon or parmesan cheese.

If you are adding chopped parsley, do it right at the

end of the cooking, otherwise the flavour of the
parsley tends to be too
strong.

A little cream added to the
eggs just before cooking is
finished will make them
extra rich.

Separating eggs

To separate eggs you can
use a small funnel over a
bowl. Break the egg over
the funnel; the white will
run through into the bowl,
the yolk will remain in the
funnel.

The old cook's way,
however, is to break the
egg into a cup, then pour
the egg into your hand over
a basin. Let the white run
through your fingers; the
yolk stays in your hand.

This method takes practice
and you must have per-
fectly clean, dry hands to
avoid getting grease or
moisture into the eggs.

Soufflés

Preheat the oven to 200°C.
For a soufflé for four, in a
saucepan melt 4 table-
spoons butter over low
heat, add 2 tablespoons
sifted plain flour and stir
for 2 minutes until blended.
Add ½ cup grated cheddar
cheese, 1 cup milk, salt,
freshly ground black
pepper and 1 teaspoon dry
mustard powder. Stir until
mixture thickens. Remove
from the heat and cool.
Separate 4 large eggs. Beat
egg yolks until light and
fluffy, stir into the milk
mixture. Whip egg whites

with a pinch of cream of tartar until soft peaks form. Fold into milk and egg yolk mixture and pile into 1-litre buttered and floured soufflé dish. Sprinkle the top with a little parmesan cheese. Turn down the oven to 180°C and bake for 30-35 minutes.

The stiffness of the egg whites is the secret of a light, well-risen soufflé.

If you want a sweet soufflé, substitute ½ cup grated dark chocolate and ¼ cup caster sugar for the cheese, and leave out the salt, pepper and mustard. Substitute caster sugar for the flour in the soufflé dish and sprinkle the top of the mixture with icing sugar.

When folding egg whites into a soufflé mixture, add them a little at a time. Turn the bowl to the right while folding, and do not over-fold or you will loose the air from the egg whites.

Fill the soufflé dish only as far as the rim or just below.

When you turn the oven on to preheat it, put in a flat baking tray. If you stand the soufflé on this to cook, it will rise more quickly.

Storing eggs

Eggs will keep for weeks in the refrigerator or in a cool place. It is important to keep the temperature constant — change in storing conditions will make eggs go bad.

Always store eggs with the pointed end down. This stops the yolk resting against the blunt end of the shell and going bad.

Never wash eggs before storing them. This destroys their natural protective coating.

Do not store eggs near uncovered strong-smelling food or chemicals. Egg shells are porous.

Keep unused egg yolks by covering them with cold water. Store in a covered container in the refrigerator up to 2 weeks.

Store whites or unshelled whole eggs in covered containers in the refrigerator. They should keep for 2-3 weeks.

To test whether eggs are fresh, place them in a bowl of cold water with a little salt added. A stale egg will rise to the surface.

Eggs with shiny surfaces are usually stale.

Leftover egg whites are useful for meringues, soufflés and pavlova.

Leftover egg yolks can be used in custards, zabaglione, hollandaise sauce, béarnaise sauce, egg and breadcrumb coatings, as soup thickeners and to enrich mashed potatoes.

If you are unsure whether eggs are raw or hard-boiled, spin them on their sides on the benchtop.

Raw eggs spin neatly; cooked ones wobble.

Zabaglione

In the top half of a double saucepan or bain marie whip 4 egg yolks and 2 tablespoons white sugar until creamy. Then put the pot over barely simmering water and continue whipping while adding 8 tablespoons marsala. The mixture will foam up. Serve in parfait glasses when it forms soft mounds.

Make sure your pot is big enough — the mixture increases greatly in size as you whip it.

Do not cook this dessert over direct heat. It must be warmed slowly.

FRUIT AND VEGETABLES

Fruit and vegetables are a very important source of vitamins, minerals and roughage. Green vegetables, for example, contain vitamins A, C and B1, calcium, iron and phosphorus. Roots and tubers, such as potatoes, contain vitamin C, protein in the skin, and are rich in carbohydrates. Fruit contains vitamins C and A, roughage and natural sugar.

When shopping for vegetables and fruit, always choose those that are in season — that is, plentiful and cheap — and never buy a leafy green that is wilted or brown, limp root vegetables or sprouting potatoes. Be careful of bagged items, particularly in the case of soft, easily perishable fruit like tomatoes and stone fruit. Choose fruit that is rich in colour.

In this chapter, there are hints on the preparation and cooking of fruit and vegetables and some tempting recipes, including desserts. It is most important to vary the fruit and vegetables you serve for both taste and health reasons. Avoid soaking fruit and vegetables before cooking — this will mean loss of valuable minerals — and try to retain the skins as the nutrients are often stored just below this outer layer.

Apples

Remember most apples now are stored in a controlled atmosphere. They will ripen very quickly at normal temperature. It's preferable to keep them in the refrigerator after purchase until you are ready to use them.

When stewing apples and other fruit, remember the less liquid you use, the more flavour left in the fruit.

A piece of lemon peel in the pan adds flavour to stewed apples.

Add chopped dates or lemon peel to apple pie filling for more flavour.

Use Granny Smith apples for cooking and salads. They are the crispest yet will soften quickly for purées and cooked apple dishes.

A few slits in apples before baking stops the skin from wrinkling.

Prepare a quick dessert by peeling and quartering 1 large Granny Smith apple. Slice the quarters lengthwise into three slices each then toss lightly in a frying pan over a moderate heat with a little butter. Sprinkle in 1 tablespoon white sugar, and stir the apples so that they can caramelise to a golden brown in the heat. Watch they don't burn. Add a little apple liqueur or brandy and flame. Serve with cream.

Apple crumble

Stew 4 large Granny Smith apples in a covered saucepan with 1 cup water and 2 tablespoons sugar. Add 2 cloves for flavouring. Fluff up the stewed apples with a fork, and put them into a greased ovenproof dish. Preheat the oven to 180°C. In a bowl, rub 2 table-

spoons butter into $^1/_2$ cup self-raising flour. Add 2 tablespoons brown sugar and mix.

Sprinkle the top of the apples with the mixture and sprinkle with 1 tablespoon desiccated coconut if desired.

Bake for 20-30 minutes, until the topping is brown and crumbly.

Asparagus

To cook asparagus, tie in bundles and cover the tips with foil. Wedge the bundles upright in a tall pan containing enough boiling water to come three-quarters of the way up the stalks so that the stalks are poached and the tips steamed.

Avocado

To store the unused portion of a cut avocado, leave the stone in place, brush the cut flesh with lemon juice and cover tightly with cling film.

To ripen avocados quickly, put them in a brown paper bag with a banana for a day.

Another method is to bury them in flour.

Bananas

Don't store bananas in the refrigerator. Ripe bananas will go black; green ones won't ripen properly after they are removed from the cold atmosphere.

Ripen green bananas by lightly wrapping them in a plastic bag together with a couple of apples.

Fry halved bananas with breakfast eggs and bacon for a special taste treat.

For an easy dessert for four, take 4 ripe bananas, slice down the centre and lie the halves in an oven-proof dish. Cover bananas with 1 tablespoon lemon juice, 2 tablespoons orange juice, 2 tablespoons rum, 2 tablespoons brown sugar, 1 teaspoon each cinnamon and nutmeg. Grate lemon and orange peel over the top, dot with 1 tablespoon butter and bake in a 180°C oven for 30-40 minutes. Serve with cream.

Another quick dessert is barbecued whole bananas

in their skins. Test for doneness with a skewer.

Beans

Do not cover beans with a lid when cooking — they will loose their colour.

French beans will stay tender if washed in warm water, not cold.

Small green beans are delicious stir fried.

Berries

All berry fruits are highly perishable. When buying fruit in punnets, always look for any sign of moisture or mould which can quickly contaminate the whole punnet.

Do not wash raspberries or strawberries unless absolutely necessary. It can spoil the flavour.

If you do wash strawberries, use a little wine instead of water. They stay crisp.

If you purée berry fruits with a little sugar they can be frozen for use as sauces or in desserts where a fruit base is required.

Make berry purée by blending a punnet of fresh ripe berries with 1/2 cup white sugar and a little lemon juice. Strain through a fine strainer to get rid of the pips. This can be used as a sauce for poached fruit, or to make ice cream or mousses.

Use this method for raspberry, strawberry and

blackberry purée. Goose-
berries and blueberries
should be lightly stewed
with sugar before puréeing.

Store strawberries in a
colander to allow the air to
circulate around them.

Serve berries with Italian
mascarpone instead of
cream for a change.

Boiling
To minimise vitamin loss,
do not use too much
water when boiling green
vegetables. Use a larger
saucepan and spread the
vegetables over the bottom,
rather than piling them up
in a small saucepan. Bring
them to the boil in a little
salted water, turn down
and cover. Simmer until
tender.

A slice of lemon or a bay
leaf in the water will reduce
the odour of boiling
cabbage, cauliflower and
brussels sprouts.

Broccoli
Sprinkle steamed broccoli
florets with toasted
almonds or serve with
hollandaise sauce.

Broccoli and
cauliflower
Boil these vegetables in a
little water so that the thick
part of the stalks is in the
water and the florets are
cooked in the steam.

Cabbage and
brussels sprouts
Add a tablespoon of sugar
or a slice of lemon to the
water when cooking

cabbage, cauliflower or brussels sprouts to kill the smell.

Poach cabbage in milk for a more delicate flavour and texture. A cup of milk added to the water when cooking cauliflower helps keep it white.

Brussels sprouts taste nicer if they are cooked in chicken stock.

Carrots

To cook carrots, peel and slice if large, leave whole if baby carrots. Bring to the boil in a little water, cover and cook until just tender. Remove the lid, add 1 tablespoon sugar and 1 dessertspoon butter and allow most of the liquid to evaporate so that the carrots are caramelised over the heat. Do not allow them to burn. Stir the carrots so that they are evenly coated in the caramel. Add salt and freshly ground black pepper, and sprinkle with chopped parsley to serve.

See also Roots and tubers

Cauliflower

A squeeze of lemon juice in the cooking water will help to keep cauliflower white.

Citrus fruits

Oranges and lemons are widely used in cooking to enhance other flavours. Try a squeeze of either in the water when stewing fruit such as apple or rhubarb.

Warm lemons and oranges before squeezing to get more juice.

Sprinkle salt on grapefruit instead of sugar. It neutralises the acid in the fruit.

Oranges and lemons should not be stored together or they will go mouldy.

Orange juice and the caramelised peel add a piquant flavour to the sauce or gravy to be served with duck, veal or pork.

Lemon and orange peel is easy to remove in fine strips if you freeze the fruit for 2 hours before peeling.

Add lemon juice and caramelised peel to the gravy served with roast chicken.

To caramelise the rind of citrus fruit, remove the rind from a fresh orange or lemon with a fine grater or potato peeler. Place peel in a saucepan with 2 tablespoons white sugar and 2 tablespoons water. Slowly bring to the boil and boil till the mixture changes colour. Remove from heat and when cool, add in the juice of the fruit.

When buying citrus fruits, feel for weight. The heavy ones have the most juice.

Corn
To remove the silk from sweet corn, dampen a paper towel or toothbrush and brush downwards on the cob.

Add a teaspoon of lemon juice to the cooking water of sweet corn a minute before taking it from the stove to keep it yellow.

If you put salt in the cooking water of corn it will toughen it.

Baste cooked corn with butter using a pastry brush to cover the cob evenly.

Cucumbers
Reduce the indigestible quality of cucumbers by slicing them and sprinkling with salt. Leave for 30 minutes then wipe off the surface liquid before using in salads.

Eggplant *(aubergine)*
Use eggplant in combination meat and vegetable dishes such as ratatouille or moussaka, as it is rather bland served on its own.

To get rid of the bitter taste of eggplant, slice it and sprinkle with salt. Leave to drain for 30 minutes on paper towels, then rinse or wipe the fluid away and pat dry before using as required.

Fennel
This bulbous vegetable has a faint flavour of anise. Its tops are used as a herb in cooking. Try this delicious baked fennel dish.

Remove the hard outer leaves from a bulb of fennel and the tough bottom of the plant. Quarter the bulb, and simmer in salted water until tender — about 10 minutes. Drain and lay the fennel pieces in an oven-proof dish. Cover with cream and grated parmesan cheese. Dot with butter and sprinkle with salt and pepper. Bake in a 200°C oven for 20 minutes until golden brown.

Fruit salad

The flavour of fruit salad is improved by a sprinkle of pepper.

Garlic

When buying garlic, choose fresh-looking bulbs with no sign of mould or shoots.

Globe artichokes

Cook the leafy heads only of this vegetable. Remove the stem and scrape away the prickly choke, found inside the leaves at the top of the head.

Test the quality of a globe artichoke by breaking off some of its leaves. If they snap off crisply, the artichoke will be tender.

Add a few drops of vinegar to the cooking water when boiling globe artichokes. This will stop them from blackening.

Globe artichokes are good served with melted butter or hollandaise sauce. *See* the chapter on soups and sauces.

Green vegetables

Store green vegetables in plastic bags in the refrigerator.

Keep celery crisp by cutting the bottom off the bunch and standing it in a shallow bowl of water in the refrigerator.

The smaller and younger the green vegetable, the less time it will take to cook and more tender and flavoursome the end result will be.

All green vegetables should be cooked as quickly as possible to reduce the vitamins lost by heat.

Refresh vegetables in cold water after cooking, drain and toss in hot melted butter.

Use the vitamin-enriched water from boiling vegetables to make gravy or a sauce for the vegetables, or add it to soups or to your stock pot.

Kiwi fruit
Peel kiwi fruit with a vegetable peeler.

Slices of kiwi fruit draped over a tough piece of meat will tenderise it in 10-15 minutes.

Lemons
Lemons smeared with candle grease will keep indefinitely. Melt a candle and rub the wax over the peel. When ready to use, crack the wax off.

Squeeze lemon juice over peeled fresh peaches or nectarines to stop them going brown and to bring out the flavour.

Use lemon juice to stop the cut surfaces of fruit and vegetables going brown.

Lemon juice is high in pectin. Use it to help set jams.

Lemon juice is a substitute for vinegar in sauces and salad dressings.

Lemon juice squeezed over grilled or fried fish will bring out the flavour.

Make a simple sauce for fish by melting 2 tablespoons butter in a pan over a moderate heat. Add 1 tablespoon chopped parsley, salt and fresh ground black pepper. Add 2 tablespoons lemon juice — the sauce will foam up. Pour over grilled or fried fish and serve immediately.

Lettuce

Keep lettuces fresh by sitting them in a shallow saucer of water in the refrigerator.

Lettuces with a firm head keep better than the leafy varieties.

Melons

Refrigerate melons only long enough to chill them or the flavour will be lost.

Mushrooms

Mushrooms should not be salted until they are cooked because this will draw out the juice.

Purée leftover mushrooms in the blender with some water, then freeze them in ice cube trays for use in stews, soups and casseroles.

Don't wash mushrooms; they go mushy and lose flavour. Wipe them with a damp cloth.

Store mushrooms in a paper bag in the refrigerator. A plastic bag will make them wilt.

Onions

If you blanch onions before using them in salads or frying them, it makes them more digestible and less odorous. Either plunge whole onions into boiling water for a couple of minutes or, if they are to be fried, slice and pour boiling water over them. Drain and dry thoroughly before frying.

To stop onions collapsing when they're roasting, cut a small cross in the stem end before cooking.

If you put onions in the refrigerator for an hour or so before use, you won't cry when you are peeling and chopping them.

If you peel onions upside down, this also reduces the output of the pungent chemical that makes you cry.

Onions will brown faster if sugar is added to the frying pan.

For a delicious accompaniment to cold poultry, ham and barbecued meats, put 500 g peeled picking onions in a large saucepan with 1 tablespoon sultanas, 1 teaspoon salt, ground black pepper, 1 bay leaf, 2 table-spoons tomato purée, 2 dessertspoons white vinegar, 1 cup water, 2 tablespoons olive oil and 2 tablespoons fine white sugar. Simmer for an hour. Serve cold, sprinkled with chopped parsley.

Oranges

To remove the pith from oranges, place them in hot water for 5 minutes. The pith will come away quite easily with the skin.

Dried orange rinds added to a pot of tea, hot chocolate or soup give a piquant, refreshing flavour.

Peaches, apricots and nectarines

It is possible to keep ripe (not soft) peaches, apricots and nectarines in the refrigerator for up to a week. They must be used immediately after removing, however.

Remember that all soft stone fruit bruises easily. Do not pile them in a bowl — store them so that they are not touching each other.

Peaches as hard as rocks can be ripened in a box covered with newspapers.

To skin a peach, put it in a pan of boiling water and count to 15 before removing and peeling it.

For a perfect summer dessert, peel ripe peaches by plunging them in boiling water — the skins will slip off easily. Then squeeze a few drops of lemon juice over the peaches and make a sugar syrup by boiling 2 tablespoons white sugar and 2 tablespoons water until it forms a syrup (don't let it caramelise). Cool, then spoon over the peaches, with 1 tablespoon brandy. Allow peaches to stand in this liquid for a couple of hours, basting them frequently.

Use dried apricots to give an extra tang to meat stuffing.

Add a couple of dried apricots to Christmas cake and pudding recipes.

When stewing apricots, add a couple of cracked apricot stones to the water. The kernels will add flavour.

Pears

Always buy firm pears. If you buy them ready to eat they will be soft by the end of the day.

Brown pears have a tough skin but are excellent baked in honey and lemon juice in the oven.

Here's a classic recipe for pears in red wine. Take 4 brown pears, then peel them but leave the stalks intact. Cut a slice off their bottoms to make them stand upright and put them in a deep saucepan. Add 2 cups red wine, $\frac{1}{2}$ cup sugar, 2 cloves and a pinch of cinnamon. Bring the liquid to the boil, cover the pan and reduce the heat to a simmer. Cook the pears for about 15-20 minutes or until soft. Carefully lift them out on to a heatproof dish and boil the liquid left in the saucepan until it reduces to 1 cup. Pour this over the pears. Serve warm or cold with cream.

Peas

To enhance the flavour of peas, add a couple of pods to the cooking water.

When cooking peas, don't cover them with a lid or they will lose their colour.

Try fresh peas cooked this unusual way. In a saucepan, lightly fry a small diced white onion and 2 lettuce leaves in 1 tablespoon butter. Add 1¹/₂ cups shelled young peas and stir briskly over heat until they turn bright green. Add 2

cups chicken stock or water and salt. Simmer for 10 minutes. Drain and sprinkle with chopped fresh parsley and freshly ground black pepper.

Potatoes

Don't forget, potatoes will go green in the light; store them in a dark place.

Don't store potatoes in plastic — they will rot.

Keep potatoes fresh longer by scraping off sprouts as they appear.

Unwashed potatoes will keep better than the washed ones.

A stiff wire brush is the best tool to clean dirt-encrusted potatoes.

Use small new potatoes for boiling or potato salad. Older potatoes contain more starch and are better for mashing and roasting.

Boil new potatoes in their skins to conserve nutrients.

Boiled potatoes retain their flavour best.

Never leave peeled potatoes soaking in cold water if you want to fry or roast them. The starch will leach out and they will loose their 'crisping' quality.

Parboil potatoes before roasting or frying them. This will make them go brown and crisp quickly on the outside and lessens the frying time.

Insert a small skewer into potatoes to be baked in the oven and leave while cooking. Heat is conducted along the skewer to the inside of the potato, lessening the cooking time.

To lift the flavour of mashed potatoes, add chopped chives, minced onion or grated cheese.

Potato special

Preheat oven to 180°C. Finely slice 1 kg potatoes and place in a shallow ovenproof dish. Pour over $1/2$ cup milk and $1/2$ cup cream. Dot with butter, sprinkle over salt freshly ground black pepper and a little nutmeg. Bake until the top is brown and the potatoes are soft.

Rhubarb

Reduce the acidity of rhubarb by cooking it in cold tea.

Roots and tubers

Potatoes, parsnips, turnips, carrots and other root and tuberous vegetables all need a longer cooking time to soften them than green vegetables.

Remove the feathery tops of carrots, parsnips and radishes to store them. The tops draw the moisture from the vegetables and cause them to wither.

Slice root and tuberous vegetables into small pieces to cut down on cooking time. Do not overcook and let them become soggy.

Always put root vegetables in cold water, not hot, to start cooking and boil with the lid on.

Steaming

Steaming is a nutritious way of cooking vegetables as vitamins and minerals are not leached out in the cooking water. It takes longer than boiling, so allow extra time — usually half as much again.

Steam light leafy vegetables such as broccoli, cabbage and cauliflower as an alternative to boiling.

Spinach

Wash spinach thoroughly before cooking. Remove as much of the stalks as possible, as these hold the grit.

To cook spinach, simply allow the leaves to wilt over a low heat in their own liquid and the washing water left on the leaves. Cool and purée leaves in the blender with a little cream, a knob of butter, salt, freshly ground black pepper and a pinch of nutmeg.

Stir-frying

To stir-fry vegetables, use enough oil to cover the bottom of a frying pan. Cut the vegetables into small pieces, then place them in the hot oil and stir and turn constantly. Fry only small batches at a time.

Tomatoes

Ripen tomatoes in a warm dark place with a ripe tomato among them. Putting them in the light will make them soft but not ripe.

Maximise the flavour of tomatoes by combining them with basil or chives.

Organically-grown and vine-ripened tomatoes are best for flavour. Buy them when you can find them.

Remove tomato skins by plunging the fruit into boiling water for 30 seconds.

If you slice tomatoes down and not across they will stay firm and not make sandwiches soggy.

Tropical fruit

Both fresh pineapple and pawpaw contain an enzyme

that breaks down protein. Do not combine these with milk or cream in any dishes as they will curdle.

Core fresh pineapple slices by pressing a small, round pastry cutter firmly over the core of each slice.

Zucchini

Small zucchini have far more flavour than large ones. Steam the large zucchini, split and remove the centre seeds, then fill the hollow inside with a tasty stuffing of cooked meat, onion and bread-crumbs. Top with flakes of butter and bake in a medium oven until heated through.

Cut small zucchini into rounds and blanch for 30 seconds in boiling water. Refresh and drain in cold water to brighten the colour and stop the cook-ing. Toss in hot butter and finish with salt, freshly ground black pepper and a sprinkle of parsley.

Use the same method to cook celery, sliced beans, snow peas and sugar snap peas.

SOUPS AND SAUCES

SOUPS AND SAUCES

In this chapter you'll find hints on how to make basic stocks, which are the basis of all good soups and essential to the flavour of casseroles and gravies. They are also used in the preparation of many sauces. Good cooks always have stock on hand. Stocks are not expensive to make — a few bones and vegetables and a large cooking pot are all you need — and they require little skill to prepare; just follow the technique outlined here.

You'll need no special equipment for basic gravy and sauce preparation, but a double saucepan is a useful item to have when you are making the more complex emulsions, such as hollandaise sauce, which require beating over gentle heat. The saucepan can double as a steamer for general use in the kitchen.

Apple sauce

To make apple sauce, wash 2 cooking apples and cut them roughly (including skin and seeds). Place them in a saucepan with 2 cloves and 2 tablespoons water and cook, covered, over a gentle heat.

When cooked, purée through a strainer with the aid of a wooden spoon. Add a little sugar if the apples are very tart.

Basic broth

Broth is a liquid containing the juices and flavours of meats and bones, with diced vegetables and a cereal added.

To make a basic broth, cut the meat from the bones of a 250 g neck of mutton or gravy beef or veal knuckle, remove any fat and dice the meat finely. Soak the meat and bones in 1 litre of water for 30 minutes.

Bring the water, meat and bones to the boil and add 2 tablespoons rice or barley as soon as it is boiling. Simmer, covered, for 1 hour.

Dice 1 stalk celery, $1/2$ medium sized turnip, $1/2$ carrot and $1/2$ onion, add them to the saucepan and simmer for a further 30 minutes. Remove fat and bones before serving.

Chocolate sauce

For an easy homemade chocolate sauce, combine 1 cup cocoa, 1 generous tablespoon golden syrup,

1 tablespoon sugar, ½ cup water, 1 tablespoon butter and 1 tablespoon rum in a heavy saucepan. Stir over low heat until ingredients are melted, then boil for 2 minutes.

Cold potato soup or Vichyssoise

In a large saucepan, melt 2 tablespoons butter and add 3 sliced and washed leeks, 1 finely chopped white onion, 2 medium-sized, peeled and diced potatoes, salt and white pepper. Cook over low heat for 10 minutes, turning the vegetables in the butter. Add 6 cups chicken stock and simmer for 20 minutes. Cool and blend to a smooth consistency or push through sieve. Add 1 cup cream. Serve cold, garnished with chives and paprika. Serves six.

Deglazing

Make an easy sauce in the pan in which you have roasted, sautéed or fried your meat. Just add ½ cup wine, stock, cream or lemon juice as appropriate over a high heat, stirring and scraping the bottom of the pan to incorporate the meat juices and scraps. This is called deglazing. Season to taste and pour over the meat or serve in a gravy boat at the table.

Gravy

Make gravy from the pan juices and dripping from roast meat to serve as an accompaniment.

Pour off all but 2 table-spoons of fat from the roasting pan, and try to retain any juices from the meat. Add 1 heaped tablespoon plain flour or cornflour and blend to incorporate the dripping and any scrapings in the pan. Gradually add 500 ml water or stock (beef, vegetable or chicken), and stir over a low heat until the gravy thickens. Season with salt and pepper. Strain into a gravy boat.

Always add warm stock or water slowly to avoid forming lumps.

If you find your gravy is too pale, add 1 teaspoon instant coffee. Use the water drained from cooking your green vegetables to make your gravy — you'll get the benefit of the vitamins in the water.

Hard sauces
Hard sauces are perfect to serve with steamed puddings. Cream 1 cup softened butter until fluffy and add 1/2 cup icing, caster or soft brown sugar and beat until it has the consistency of whipped cream. Gradually add 2 tablespoons of either rum, brandy, fruit purée or coffee essence. Then beat in another tablespoon sugar. Refrigerate until needed.

Hollandaise sauce
This delicious sauce is served with fish and vegetables. Like other

emulsion sauces, it is made by beating egg yolks with butter over a low heat.

Here is a quick and easy way to make hollandaise sauce. Soften ½ cup butter in the top of a double saucepan or container over simmering water (the water must not touch the bottom of the container). In a separate bowl or glass jug beat 3 egg yolks, gradually adding 1½ tablespoons lemon juice.

Then very slowly add the egg yolk mixture to the melting butter, stirring vigorously with a wooden spoon until the sauce reaches coating consistency. Season with pepper and salt if desired.

You must not overheat the mixture as the egg yolk will overcook and curdle.

A poached egg on toast topped with hollandaise sauce makes a gourmet brunch.

Mayonnaise

Mayonnaise is made by combining egg yolks and oil to form an emulsion. A little vinegar is added to give it tang.

When making mayonnaise, all your ingredients must be at room temperature or the mixture won't thicken.

Lightly beat an egg yolk in a glass bowl until it is creamy, adding 1 teaspoon French mustard. Then, one drip at a time, add 1 cup good-quality olive oil to the yolk, beating briskly with a wooden spoon or in the mixer to form an emulsion. The mixture should quickly thicken and become very creamy. Continue slowly adding oil, beating all the time, and then add 1 dessertspoon vinegar or lemon juice drop by drop to thin the mixture as needed. Season with salt and pepper.

The mayonnaise will not thicken if the oil is added too quickly to the egg yolk.

Mayonnaise will keep for up to a week in the refrigerator in a covered container.

Combine mayonnaise with chopped chives, parsley,

dill or other herbs to serve in salads or with cold vegetables, poultry or fish.

Add 1 tablespoon chopped capers and 1 tablespoon chopped gherkins to mayonnaise to make tartare sauce to serve with fried or grilled fish.

If your mayonnaise won't thicken or it curdles, spoon off the oil from the top of the mixture and beat in an extra egg yolk (room temperature). Then commence adding oil again, drop by drop, while beating.

Another trick for rescuing a curdled mixture is to take a clean bowl and beat the mixture in it with a teaspoon of iced water or sliver of ice.

Pumpkin soup

One of the simplest soups to make, pumpkin soup is a nourishing light meal or entrée.

In a large saucepan, lightly fry 2 medium-sized peeled and chopped onions in 2 tablespoons butter. Add 2 cups cubed pumpkin and sauté in the butter. Add 6 cups chicken stock, salt and freshly ground black pepper. Bring to the boil then simmer, covered, until pumpkin is tender. Cool and purée or blend until smooth. Reheat and serve garnished with cream and grated nutmeg or mace.

To thicken any vegetable soups without using cream, take a cup of the soup, purée it in the blender and return it to the pot.

As a pick-me-up for a dull soup, add a dessertspoon or two of dry sherry before serving.

Salty soup

If soup is too salty, try lowering a lump of sugar on a spoon into the pot for a moment.

Or if you are making a white soup, replace a cup of the soup with a cup of milk to dilute the salt.

Stock

Put at least 1 kg assorted bones and carcasses into a large saucepan with 2 litres water, 1 sliced onion, 1 peeled and sliced carrot, 1 sliced stalk celery, 1 bay leaf, 1 sprig parsley, salt and a few black peppercorns.

Bring to boil, skim, cover tightly, reduce heat and simmer for 1-1½ hours. Cool and strain.

Slice or dice vegetables for the stock pot for maximum flavour.

Always make stock and soup before you need it so that you can remove the fat from the surface after it has solidified.

Egg shells added to stock will attract the scum on the surface. Lift out the shells to clarify the stock.

For chicken stock, use chicken carcasses or bones and feet. (Feet are good for thickening as they contain

gelatin.) For an extra-rich stock use a boiling fowl.

For beef stock, use beef bones and include a marrow bone, which contains gelatin, for thickening. For an extra-rich stock use a beef shin or some gravy beef and brown it first in a little butter.

For fish stock, use fish heads and bones. A little white wine adds flavour.

For vegetable stock, use carrots, parsnips, jerusalem artichokes, turnips, onions, leeks and any green vegetables such as peas or beans.

Add any water in which you have cooked vegetables to your stockpot, along with washed outside leaves of lettuce or cauliflower.

Don't let the liquid boil continuously when making stock — it will go cloudy. Just simmer.

If you have added too much salt to soup or stock by mistake, add a few slices of raw potato. The potato will absorb the salt and you can remove it before serving the soup.

Stock can be reheated to boiling, skimmed and strained again and then used to make soups, gravies and sauces.

Save all chicken, beef and veal bones from roasts and grills to go in the stock pot.

An instant thickener for soups is a little boiled rice.

Stock — storing

Store stock in small quantities in plastic containers in the freezer.

Line measuring cups with freezer bags, pour the stock into the bags, lift out, seal and freeze in this handy size.

Always label your stocks clearly so you know the type and date.

Reduce your stock right down to a strong extract by simmering. Then pour it into ice cube trays to freeze it until you need it as a base for sauces or to give flavour to soups and casseroles.

The frozen cubes can be added to soups and casseroles without being defrosted.

Vegetable soup or minestrone

In a large saucepan, lightly fry a chopped rasher of bacon and a sliced onion in 1 tablespoon oil. Add a peeled, diced carrot, ½ peeled, diced turnip, 1 diced stalk celery, 1 diced potato and 1 tablespoon haricot beans which have been soaked overnight. Add 5 cups chicken stock, bring to boil and simmer for 30 minutes, then add 4 tablespoons assorted dried pasta and 1 tablespoon rice. Simmer gently for 30 minutes then add 4 tablespoons sliced French beans and ¾ cup chopped cabbage. Add salt and pepper to taste and simmer for another 10 minutes. Serves six, garnished with chopped ham and grated parmesan cheese.

White sauce

From a basic white sauce you can create many variations to serve with different dishes.

Make a roux with 2 tablespoons melted butter and 2 tablespoons plain flour. Stir over low heat until well blended. Gradually add 2 cups warm milk or 1 cup milk and 1 cup chicken stock. Add salt and white pepper to taste. Cook over low heat, stirring until mixture thickens.

You must add the liquid slowly or the mixture will form lumps.

If white sauce is lumpy strain it or blend for 30 seconds and then strain it.

Be sure not to let the butter catch and the roux go brown while you are cooking the foundations of the sauce.

Cook the roux over low heat for at least 2 minutes to get rid of the floury taste before adding the liquid.

White sauce — variations

Add 1 tablespoon capers and 1 tablespoon pickling liquid from the capers to make caper sauce.

Add 2 tablespoons grated cheese and a pinch of cayenne to make cheese sauce. Cover steamed vegetables such as cauliflower or leeks with this sauce and brown under the griller or in the oven to make dishes au gratin.

Add 2 tablespoons French mustard, or 1 tablespoon made-up English mustard and 1 tablespoon white vinegar, to make mustard sauce, the traditional accompaniment to boiled salted meats.

Lie steamed and boned chicken pieces in an ovenproof casserole dish, pour over white sauce made with half chicken stock (*see* white sauce recipe) and top with bacon rashers or breadcrumbs dotted with butter. Reheat in a moderate oven.

A dessertspoon of dry sherry added to the sauce gives this extra flavour.

Or you can add sautéed button mushrooms or drained tinned asparatus pieces to the chicken.

Substitute tinned salmon or tuna for the chicken pieces for another simple dish using white sauce. If you use cheese sauce it is even better.

SALADS

Salads should be part of our daily diet. Since they are usually composed of raw vegetables, fruits and herbs, the high mineral and vitamin content of these foods is not spoiled by cooking and they are therefore highly nutritious.

Salad ingredients need to be of excellent quality as imperfections cannot be disguised by cooking. Salads must look appetising and appealing, so your presentation dishes are important. If you use a wooden salad bowl, don't wash it in detergent and water; wipe it out with paper towels and keep it well seasoned with oil. You should have several attractive glass bows in your cupboard so that the blend and colours of mixed salads can be appreciated at the table. Salad bowls should not be too shallow to allow for tossing, unless the recipe is one that calls for ingredients to soak or marinate.

Wash salad greens well to get rid of dirt and insects. A plastic lettuce dryer that operates by spinning the water off is a great help. Otherwise drain the greens well in a wire basket, strainer or in a cloth.

In this chapter there are some tried and true salad recipes and suggestions for tempting dressings.

Basics

Successful salads depend on fresh, crisp vegetables. Keep lettuce wrapped in paper rather than plastic bags which tend to make it rust. If you are using plastic bags, line the bottom of the bag with paper towels to absorb excess moisture.

Wash lettuce and dry well in a cloth or drain in a wire basket or strainer before dressing the salad. If there is any water on the leaves the dressing will not cling but run to the bottom of the bowl.

To keep it crisp, keep your salad in the refrigerator until you are ready to serve it.

Lemon juice keeps salad oil and vinegar from separating, so add a few drops when you are making a vinaigrette dressing.

Remember if you are making a salad to accompany other food as a side dish, or if the salad is to be an entrée, don't include ingredients in your salad that are already part of the menu. For example, don't include tomatoes in the salad if you are serving spaghetti bolognese which is made with tomatoes!

Toasted sesame seeds and toasted pine nuts add great crunch to salads.

Don't overdo the garlic. Remember, not everyone likes it. Try rubbing the salad bowl with garlic for a more subtle flavour instead of including it in the dressing.

Tear the lettuce leaves rather than cutting them. Cutting can leave a brown edge and make the leaves limp.

Tear salad leaves into bite-size pieces for easier eating!

Raw onion in salads upsets the digestion; use paper-thin slices of Spanish onion instead.

Celery curls
Make attractive garnishes to decorate your salads. Take a head of celery and cut the stalks into 10-cm pieces. From one end make 3 or 4 parallel cuts down each piece, about 6 cm long. Do not cut too far down. Put the celery pieces into the refrigerator in a bowl of cold water. As the water becomes colder, the cut ends of the pieces will turn up, making attractive curls.

Coleslaw
Combine 2 cups finely shredded cabbage, ½ cup diced celery, ¼ cup grated Granny Smith apple, 1

tablespoon shredded coconut and a handful of sultanas in a salad bowl. Blend 1/4 cup mayonnaise (*see* the chapter on soups and sauces) with 1/4 cup basic French dressing; toss through salad. Season with salt and freshly ground black pepper.

The dressing should be added about an hour before serving.

A spicy alternative is to use thousand island dressing.

Cucumber

Cucumber is good combined with plain yoghurt and makes an excellent accompaniment to spicy dishes. Peel and slice the cucumber and sprinkle with salt. Leave bitter moisture to drain from the slices then pat dry. Add 1/2 cup yoghurt combined with a crushed clove of garlic and 1 teaspoon dried or fresh chopped mint and mix through the cucumber slices. Sprinkle with salt, freshly ground black pepper and garnish with sprigs of fresh mint.

Dressing

For a creamy finish to a salad dressing, slowly add the oil to the other ingredients, using the blender.

Another way to make a creamy dressing is to add an ice cube to the dressing while you are blending it. Remove the cube immediately after the dressing is mixed.

Use lemon juice in your basic French dressing if fish is part of the salad.

Make your own collection of herb oils to use in cooking and dressings. Simply add good-quality warm olive oil to crushed fresh leaves of herbs and leave for a few days to infuse. Drain and bottle.

Use the same method to make herb vinegars. Warm the vinegar slightly before pouring it on to the herbs. Don't use an aluminium saucepan as the vinegar will stain it.

Add dressings to green salads just before serving.

Add dressing to potato salad when you make it — preferably when the

potatoes are still warm and will absorb the dressing.

French dressing or vinaigrette

In the blender or screw-topped jar combine 1 cup olive oil and 1/2 cup white vinegar with a crushed clove of garlic, salt and freshly ground black pepper. Blend ingredients thoroughly.

Change the basic ingredients to suit your salad. You can use virgin olive oil, which has a stronger flavour, or a herbed olive oil, or red wine or balsamic vinegar to give your dressings a kick.

You can also use the vinegar from jars of gherkins or pickles for extra flavour.

Another way to add interest to French dressing is to use chilli sauce (add it a little at a time and taste carefully).

Use lemon juice in your basic French dressing if fish is part of the salad.

Green vegetables

Any green vegetable can be used in salads. Blanch sliced zucchini, green beans and broccoli florets in boiling water for 15 seconds, refresh under cold water and drain thoroughly. Use snow peas raw.

Combine 1 cup each sliced blanched and drained zucchini, green beans and broccoli florets, with 1 cup snow peas. Pour over 1/2 cup basic French dressing while vegetables are still warm and sprinkle with chopped fresh mint or basil.

Ham, apple and potato salad

Put 1/2 cup mayonnaise (*see* the chapter on soups and sauces) into a salad bowl. Add 2 cups diced boiled new potatoes, 1 diced Granny Smith apple, 2 cups diced celery and 1 cup cooked diced ham. Season with salt and freshly ground black pepper and scatter 1/4 cup chopped fresh tarragon over the salad.

This salad must be dressed immediately it is made. The lemon juice in the mayonnaise will stop the cut apple going brown.

Marinated mushroom salad

Place 3 cups button mushrooms in a shallow china or glass dish. In a bowl combine 1 clove crushed garlic, 1/4 cup lemon juice, 1 teaspoon French mustard and 1 cup olive oil.

Blend well, pour over the mushrooms and leave them to soak for at least 6 hours, turning occasionally.

Scatter a little chopped parsley over before serving and add more freshly ground black pepper.

Mushrooms absorb a lot of oil — you may need to add a little more during the soaking process.

Oils

The best oil to use in making dressings is top-quality olive oil.

Virgin olive oil is made from the first pressing of the olives and is much stronger in flavour than the oil from the later pressings.

You can pick it by its green colouring; oil from later pressings is a lighter golden colour.

Use virgin olive oil wherever recipes stipulate olive oil if you like the flavour.

However, it does tend to overpower some salads, so experiment. Use oil from the later pressings if the virgin oil is too strong.

Oil does not last indefinitely. It is important to store it away from heat.

Use lighter oils such as peanut and safflower for cooking, never in the preparation of salad dressings.

Pasta shell salad

Toss together 2 cups cooked pasta shells, 1 cup chopped ham, ½ cup sliced celery and ¼ cup chopped spring onions. Dress with ¼ cup mayonnaise (*see* the chapter on soups and sauces) with 1 teaspoon horseradish added and season with salt and freshly ground black pepper. Garnish with chopped parsley and tomato quarters.

Pears vinaigrette

Fruit combined with a tart or spicy dressing can make an excellent entrée or appetiser before a heavy main course.

Peel, core and slice 4 firm but ripe pears. Prepare a quantity of basic French dressing and add a few drops of lemon juice and 1 teaspoon dry mustard powder.

Pour this over the pears and toss them in 2 tablespoons chopped fresh mint and 2 tablespoons chopped fresh parsley. Season with salt and freshly ground black pepper to taste.

Use a walnut-flavoured oil to make the dressing to give it an unusual flavour.

Pulses

Use cooked pulses such as lentils and haricot or lima beans spiced with herbs and vinaigrette dressing in your salads.

Soak 1 cup lima beans overnight in cold water, then cook beans till tender (about 2 hours). Drain thoroughly and add ½ cup cooked whole round stringless or French beans. Dress with ¼ cup basic French dressing mixed with ¼ cup plain yoghurt and chopped herbs, salt and freshly ground black pepper or cayenne pepper.

Radish roses

Make radish roses by cutting a slice off the top and bottoms of round radishes. Then, using a sharp knife, gash the radish to make petals starting near the root and working up in rows going round the radish. Put the radishes in a bowl of water in the refrigerator. The iced water will cause the points to open up and curl back where they have been cut.

Rice salad

Mix 2 cups warm rice with 1 small tin tuna, 1 table-spoon chopped tinned anchovies, the oil from the tuna and anchovies, 2 quar-tered hard-boiled eggs, 2 quartered tomatoes, 1 tablespoon black olives and 1 tablespoon each chopped chives and parsley. Dress with 1 tablespoon white vinegar and season with freshly ground black pepper.

Roquefort dressing

Add 2-4 tablespoons crumbled roquefort cheese to 1 cup French dressing and beat well. Keep chilled until ready to use.

This dressing goes well with mixed salad greens or baby spinach leaves. If roquefort cheese is hard to get, crumble some firm blue vein cheese into the dressing instead.

Salad niçoise

A simple salad can make a delicious light meal or entrée. You can make this one hours in advance and keep it chilled in the refrigerator until ready to use.

Place a quantity of French dressing (made with lemon juice instead of vinegar) in the bottom of a large glass or plastic salad bowl.

Arrange on top well-washed lettuce leaves, tuna pieces (tinned or grilled fresh), 1/2 cup chopped cooked green beans, 4 small quartered tomatoes, 2 sliced hard-boiled eggs, 1 tablespoon chopped green pepper, 1/2 cup black olives, 2 sliced radishes and 1/4 cup chopped anchovies.

Toss the salad carefully to incorporate the dressing and garnish with chopped parsley, salt and freshly ground black pepper.

Spinach salad

Use 200 g baby spinach leaves for this salad and wash them thoroughly. Place the leaves in a salad bowl. Fry 2 rashers chopped bacon until crisp, cool and add to the spinach. Pour over ½ cup roquefort dressing and top with 2 tablespoons croûtons (diced stale bread, fried in the bacon fat until crisp).

If you warm ⅓ cup French dressing instead of the roquefort and pour it over baby spinach leaves, it makes an interesting variation.

Spring onion flowers

To make spring onion flowers, use about 8 cm of the root end of the onion. Remove any papery outside skin.

Grip the root end and, using a sharp knife, cut the stem lengthwise two or three times to within 2.5 cm of the root end.

Place in a bowl of cold water in the refrigerator to curl.

Thousand island dressing

Mix 1 cup mayonnaise (*see* the chapter on soups and sauces) with 1 tablespoon chilli sauce and 1 teaspoon worcestershire sauce. Finish with a teaspoon chopped chives. Keep chilled.

This rich and spicy dressing is good served with chicken or coleslaw salads.

Tomato and basil salad

Slice juicy red tomatoes and lie them in a shallow serving dish. Slice bocconcini (small mozzarella cheeses) and lie a piece on the top of each tomato slice. Drizzle with virgin olive oil and a little herb vinegar. Scatter plenty of torn fresh basil over and season with salt and freshly ground black pepper.

If you add some sliced avocado to this dish, it makes a perfect summer entrée.

Little bell-shaped tomatoes give an unusual finish to a salad.

Tossing

Some cooks swear that the best way to toss a salad is by hand. Turn the salad over carefully to ensure the dressing coats the leaves evenly.

Tropical fruit salad

Place in a large china or glass salad bowl 2 cups diced fresh pineapple, 2 cups diced fresh pawpaw, 1 cup sliced mangoes, 2 cups watermelon scooped out with a melon baller, 2 sliced bananas and add 2 tablespoons Kirsch or Maraschino liqueur and sugar to taste.

Variations

Unsalted cashews, toasted pine nuts, sesame seeds, walnuts or macadamias add great crunch to any salad.

Waldorf salad

This salad makes an ideal lunch and uses up leftover cold chicken.

To serve six, mix together 2 cups diced cold chicken, 1 peeled and sliced stalk celery, 1 diced Granny Smith apple (leave the skin on), 15 whole walnuts, broken in halves and 1 cup mayonnaise made with lemon juice (*see* the chapter on soups and sauces).

Season with salt and freshly ground black pepper and spoon into lettuce leaves to serve.

Warm potato salad

Boil whole new potatoes in their skins until tender.

Drain and slide skins off.

Chop potatoes roughly and add ¼ cup chopped cooked bacon. Dress with mayonnaise, thinned with a little basic French dressing and season with salt and freshly ground black pepper. Garnish with ¼ cup of either chopped chives, torn basil leaves or chopped dill.

An alternative to mayonnaise in this salad is to use yoghurt combined with basic French dressing.

Leave the skins on Desirée potatoes, cut them into quarters and boil them for a new-look potato salad. The skins are pink and the flesh is pale yellow.

Don't overcook potatoes for potato salad or they will collapse, lose their skin and not hold the dressing.

PASTA AND RICE

PASTA AND RICE

Pasta and rice are easily digestible, energy-providing, high carbohydrate foods that are ideal in combination with other foods or delicious simply served with butter and herbs and seasonings. To cook both pasta and rice you will need large saucepans. Rice swells during cooking to at least three times its dry size and spaghetti and macaroni both double in size. And, importantly, you must cook pasta in a large quantity of water to allow it to cook evenly. Make sure you have a large colander, preferably one that stands on its own legs, to drain it.

The most common commercially available pasta is the dried variety made from flour and water. You can also buy dried pasta which contains eggs, and the fresh soft egg pasta is also widely available — or you can make your own. Fresh pasta is perishable. It must be kept refrigerated and will not last longer than about 2 weeks. Dried pasta will last indefinitely in its packet or a glass jar in the cupboard. White rice is the most commonly used variety and keeps almost indefinitely if stored in a screw-topped jar so that weevils and other pests can't attack it. Brown rice is less processed than white and doesn't keep as long.

The culinary combinations using pasta and rice are endless. Here are some basic hints and suggestions that will help you to make the most of them.

Pasta cooking

To cook dried spaghetti or other long varieties, put the ends in first and push down into the boiling water gently with a spoon. Do not break the strands.

Add pasta to boiling water gradually, so the water does not go off the boil.

Don't try to cook too much pasta at once. It is better to do it in several saucepans than overcrowd and risk the pasta not cooking fast

or evenly, or becoming gluey.

A useful rule of thumb is 2 litres of water to every 250 g pasta.

Add a dessertspoon of oil to the cooking water before you add the pasta to stop it sticking together.

Cooking times will vary according to the shape of the pasta, and whether it is dried or fresh. Chunky shapes may take longer than thin noodles. The longest you should ever have to cook dried pasta is 15 minutes.

Pasta will continue to soften after you drain it after cooking.

Pasta with cream sauce

Melt ½ cup pure cream with 2 tablespoons butter in a heavy heatproof casserole. Stir gently until the sauce thickens. Cook enough pasta for four people in boiling salted water, drain and add to the cream sauce. Toss the pasta over a low heat to coat it with the sauce. Add another ½ cup cream, ½ cup grated parmesan cheese and toss again. Season well with freshly ground black

pepper and sprinkle with grated nutmeg and serve immediately.

This cream sauce is perfect for fettuccine.

Pasta — dried

To cook dried pasta bring a large saucepan of water to the boil, add 1 dessert-spoon (at least) of salt and 1 teaspoon olive oil and drop the pasta carefully into the water.

Cover the saucepan until the water is boiling again, then remove the lid.

Cook at a fast boil, stirring occasionally with a wooden spoon to stop the pasta sticking until *al dente*, that is, until still firm but malleable.

Turn out immediately into a colander and drain off all the water to stop the cooking process.

If you wish, you can add a cup of cold water to the saucepan before turning out the pasta to stop it cooking any further.

Put the pasta into a warm serving bowl and add butter, freshly grated parmesan cheese or toss with a sauce and serve immediately.

Allow 100-120 g dried pasta per person.

Pasta — fresh

Fresh pasta made with eggs is cooked in exactly the same way as dried but for half the time or less. Very fresh spaghetti should only take 2 or 3 minutes.

Filled chunky pasta like ravioli or tortellini will take longer to cook than unfilled.

Pasta with homemade tomato sauce

In a large saucepan, simmer together 4 cups ripe peeled tomatoes, 1 large peeled diced carrot, 1 sliced stalk celery and 1 peeled diced onion for about 20-30 minutes. Cool and purée the mixture and keep in the refrigerator until ready to use.

Use this sauce on fettuccine. Top with torn basil leaves and freshly grated parmesan cheese.

Pasta with meat sauce

In a heavy pan soften 1 peeled and chopped onion, 1 sliced stalk celery, 1 peeled and chopped clove garlic and 1 peeled and chopped carrot in 2 tablespoons olive oil. Add 2 cups minced beef and brown lightly. Add a bay leaf, 2 tablespoons chopped herbs (tarragon, thyme, parsley and basil), 2 cups drained tinned tomatoes or homemade tomato purée and 1/2 cup red wine.

Season with salt and pepper. Simmer over low heat for 20 minutes.

Don't over-brown the meat in this sauce. It should just change colour before you add the other ingredients.

Use this meat sauce to serve with fettuccine or as a filling for a baked lasagne.

You can add 2 tablespoons cream to the sauce before serving to give it extra richness.

Pasta with oil and garlic sauce

This fragrant sauce goes well with spaghetti.

Put your spaghetti on to cook in plenty of boiling salted water. Heat a pan with 1/2 cup olive oil and 1 teaspoon salt. Sauté 2 peeled and finely chopped cloves garlic over a low heat. Do not burn. When the pasta is *al dente*, drain and toss in the garlic-flavoured oil. Season with plenty of freshly ground black pepper and serve with grated parmesan cheese.

Pasta and parmesan cheese

Freshly grated parmesan cheese is preferable to commercially grated. Try to buy parmesan in the piece; otherwise use a chunk of cheddar or gruyère to grate over your pasta dishes.

Never offer cheese with pasta dishes that contain fish.

Pasta with pesto sauce

Combine 2 cloves peeled chopped garlic, 6 tablespoons torn fresh basil leaves, 1/4 cup pine nuts and 1/2 cup grated fresh parmesan in a blender.

Gradually add 3 tablespoons olive oil and season with salt and freshly ground black pepper.

Use this sauce to serve on tagliatelle or spaghetti. Add a tablespoon or so of boiling water from pasta to heat it before adding to the pasta.

Pasta — serving

Most pasta dishes are fairly substantial. If pasta is on the menu, make sure you have light courses to serve before or after.

Serve pasta in bowls with a curved edge or in shallow soup plates, so that sauces do not run over the edge and can be scooped up easily.

Serve crusty bread with pasta to mop up sauces.

Make sure everyone is seated at the table before you drain the pasta. It must be eaten hot.

Pasta — varieties

Flat pasta varieties include fettuccine (noodles about 3 mm wide), tagliatelle (about 6 mm wide) and lasagne, which is used in combination with meat sauce and cheese. Flat noodles are best served with meat or tomato sauces.

Round noodles include spaghetti and the thinner spaghettini. They go well with oil and garlic sauces.

Stuffed pasta includes ravioli, tortellini and cannelloni. They are good topped with meat or cream sauces.

Other pasta shapes include bucatini (thick wide spaghetti, good with tomato and garlic sauces); conchiglie (little shells, good with all sauces); penne (feathers, good with tomatoes); and macaroni (short, fat tubes, good with meat and cheese sauces).

Rice

Short-grained rice is more inclined to stick together than long-grained. It is ideal for Chinese cookery and easy to eat with chopsticks.

Long-grained rice is slightly more fluffy after cooking.

Brown or wholemeal rice has some of the husks on the rice. It takes longer to cook than white rice and contains more fibre, fat, minerals and vitamins. It also has a more interesting flavour than white rice.

To reduce the cooking time of brown rice, soak it for 12 hours in water before cooking.

Wild rice is the seed of a wild grass. It is much more expensive than rice.

Remember that rice expands to three times its dry size when cooked.

Rinse rice thoroughly before cooking, not after, otherwise you'll wash away the vitamins and nutrients in the cooking water.

Steam rice using the absorption method (*see* Steamed rice).

Always stir rice with a fork; spoon stirring makes it mushy.

Add a teaspoon of oil to the saucepan when cooking rice — it stops the grains sticking together.

A squeeze of lemon juice added to the cooking water will keep rice white.

Reheat small quantities of cooked boiled rice in the top of a vegetable steamer or in a strainer over boiling water.

The easily digestible qualities of boiled rice make it an ideal invalid or breakfast food.

Finely chopped coriander gives cooked rice an Asian flavour.

Add rice to soups and casseroles as a thickener.

Rice cooked in chicken or vegetable stock has a delicious flavour.

Store uncooked rice in clean, dry airtight containers in a cool place.

Store cooked rice in a sealed container in the refrigerator for 5-7 days. Reheat over simmering water or use it to make rice salad, fried rice or stuffing.

Cooked rice may be frozen for 2-3 months.

Rice pilaf
Wash 1½ cups rice thoroughly in several rinses.

In a large saucepan, melt 1 tablespoon butter and soften a chopped white onion. Add rice and stir over a low heat till grains are coated, then add 3 cups chicken stock or water and bring to boil. Turn the heat right down, cover saucepan and simmer until the liquid has been absorbed.

Serve rice pilaf with casseroles, chicken dishes, curries and fish.

Rice porridge
This Asian dish is easy to digest and makes an ideal invalid meal.

Wash 2 cups short-grained rice thoroughly, drain, stir in 1 dessertspoon peanut oil and mix thoroughly through the rice. Bring 5 cups chicken stock to the boil and add the rice. Turn the heat down as low as possible, cover the sauce-pan and simmer for 2 hours until the rice has become a creamy porridge.

Serve this with a little chopped bacon, soy sauce, some roasted almonds and chopped spring onions as condiments.

Risotto

The secret of cooking risotto successfully is to add the liquid gradually and to stir constantly so that it is absorbed evenly. This will produce a creamy finish without sogginess.

The rice grains must remain separate in risotto dishes.

You must use the more expensive arborio rice to make a genuine risotto. It is available at supermarkets and Italian food stores.

Use a large shallow pan. Sauté 1 small chopped white onion in 2 table-spoons butter. Add 2 cups arborio rice and stir until coated with butter. In a saucepan, bring 8 cups chicken stock to the boil. Add ½ cup stock to the rice and stir thoroughly until the liquid is absorbed. Continue to add simmering stock to the rice by ¼ cups, stirring constantly so that the rice doesn't stick to the pan and absorbs the liquid evenly. Continue the process until rice is cooked but not broken down.

Risotto is delicious simply served with freshly grated parmesan cheese. Or you can add sautéed quartered fennel bulb, or sautéed mushrooms, or melt cheese through the risotto, or toss in chopped asparagus.

Steamed rice

Use the absorption method to cook rice. It's foolproof.

Allow ½ cup uncooked rice per person. Place rice in a large saucepan and wash in cold water. Move the saucepan around until the water becomes cloudy, then pour it off carefully without losing any rice down the plug hole.

Repeat this process a number of times, adding fresh water until the water is no longer cloudy. Then cover rice with water to about 2 cm above its level in the pot. Bring rice to a rapid boil and give it a stir. Cover the saucepan, then turn the heat down to medium and simmer until the water is absorbed and little holes appear on the surface. Now turn the heat right down, as low as it will go, cover the saucepan and simmer for another 10 minutes.

This method means that all the cooking liquid is absorbed in the rice, saving all the valuable nutrients.

It leaves a crust on the bottom of the saucepan but the rest of the rice is steamed to perfection.

Stir-fried rice

For a quick and delicious snack for two, heat 1 tablespoon peanut oil in a wok or frying pan and pour in 2 lightly beaten eggs. Cook to a flat omelette. Remove eggs and set aside. Fry 2 chopped rashers bacon in the oil and add in 2 cups cold precooked boiled rice and stir-fry, making sure it is evenly cooked and has no lumps.

Add ½ cup cooked peas, the omelette cut into thin strips and ¼ cup chopped spring onions. Season with 1 tablespoon soy sauce and freshly ground black pepper.

Leave out the bacon and substitute diced vegetables (blanch them first in boiling water for 10-15 seconds, rinse under cold water, drain and dry), bean shoots and mushrooms for a stir-fried vegetarian dish.

A little fresh ginger, peeled and sliced, is delicious in stir-fried dishes.

CAKES AND PASTRY

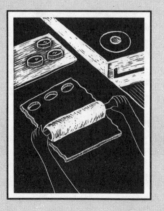

This chapter is all about baking techniques — using your oven to make cakes, biscuits, pastry and bread. Successful baking depends on dry heat causing an aerating agent to swell in a flour mixture so that the mixture stretches and rises. Temperature control is important so to regulate the process if necessary, so you must have a reliable oven.

If you like baking, it's worth spending a little time and money on the equipment to help you. The most essential item is an electric beater/blender. These range in price and capability from a simple hand-held machine to the top-of-the-range food processor which can perform so many kitchen tasks: blending, chopping, puréeing, extracting juice, making dough and creaming shortening and sugar.

You will also need wire racks on which to cool the products of your labour, and a range of cake tins to cook them in: a large square or round tin (18-20 cm), a rectangular loaf pan, a round springform tin (18-20 cm), a scone or biscuit tray and sponge pans. You should also have a flour sifter. Purists insist that egg whites are beaten with a wire whisk in a copper bowl.

Biscuits

Biscuit mixtures should always be very stiff so that the biscuits keep their shapes while cooking.

Biscuits should be cooked rather slowly so that they will be firm and crisp.

Cool biscuits on a wire rack. Don't place them in containers until they are quite cold or they will become soggy.

If you find it difficult to roll out biscuit dough thinly, chill the dough slightly and roll out between sheets of non-stick kitchen paper.

This is preferable to adding extra flour in an attempt to stop sticking, because the flour will make the mixture tough.

When shaping biscuits with your hands, moisten your hands if the dough sticks.

Have all biscuits even in size and rolled to the same thickness for overall browning.

Use a flat baking tray with low sides, because high sides prevent browning.

Some biscuits, such as those made with syrup or honey, are still soft when removed from the oven, so allow them to sit for a few minutes before transferring them from the tray to the cooling rack.

Be careful not to use too much dough for each biscuit when spooning biscuits on to a baking tray because most biscuits spread a lot during baking.

For quick and easy biscuits, preheat oven to 160°C. Sift ½ cup self-raising flour and ½ cup cornflour with a pinch of salt. Cream ½ cup butter with ¼ cup icing sugar.

Add flour and 1 teaspoon vanilla essence and mix thoroughly. Put dessert-spoons of mixture on a greased oven tray and bake for 15 minutes.

If plain biscuits become less crisp during storage, place them on a baking tray in a 170°C oven for 5 minutes. Be careful not to overbrown them.

Biscuits freeze very well. Pack them in rigid containers with well-fitting lids or freeze the uncooked dough rolled up in foil.

Bread

The basic ingredients of bread dough are plain flour, yeast, shortening in the form of butter or lard, salt, warm water or milk and sometimes a little sugar which helps the action of the yeast.

The aerating agent in bread is yeast. After combination with the sugar and warm water in the flour mixture, which is kneaded into a dough, the cells in the yeast multiply or ferment, producing carbon dioxide gas which stretches the yeast cells making them light and spongy. This is the 'rising' process.

During this process, the mixture is left in a warm, dark place. This helps the action of the yeast cells.

When the mixture has about doubled in size through the yeast action, the dough is kneaded again to distribute the air holes evenly throughout. It is then put into its greased baking tins and left to 'prove' for a time — that is, until the rising is complete. It is then baked in a hot oven, which kills the yeast cells and prevents any further rising.

Bread — basic recipe

Preheat the oven to 220°C. Take 2 kg plain flour and sift it with $1^{1}/_{4}$ tablespoons salt into a large warm basin. Make a well in the centre. Cream 30 g compressed yeast with 1 teaspoon sugar, then gradually add 4 cups lukewarm water. Pour this into the well in the flour, stirring gently until the flour is incorporated. Sprinkle the top of the batter with the last of the flour, cover with a cloth and leave until bubbles break through the surface — about 30 minutes.

When well risen, knead the mixture, first in the bowl and then on a floured board. Return it to a warm floured bowl, cover and leave in a warm, draught-free place until the mixture has doubled in size — about 2 hours.

Take out of the bowl and knead again on a floured board to distribute the air bubbles evenly. Shape into loaves, or half fill greased loaf tins and allow to stand for another 15 minutes to rise again in a warm place.

Bake for 40-60 minutes, until the loaves are a good colour.

Bread — tips
Fresh compressed yeast is best for bread making,

dried yeast may be used for buns.

Be careful that water added to the yeast is not too hot (it will kill the yeast cells), or too cold (it will have no effect on the yeast).

Warm your mixing bowl, utensils and flour before you add the yeast.

Make sure you have a warm, draught-free place for the dough to rise.

Bread dough will rise faster inside a greased plastic bag, but the flavour suffers in the process.

You'll need a floured board to mix the yeast through the flour to a dough consistency. It should not be sticky — add more flour if it is. If it seems too dry, add a little more warm water.

When baking time is over, knock the loaves gently to see if they are done — they should sound hollow.

Compressed yeast will keep for up to 2 weeks wrapped in foil in the refrigerator.

Cakes

Making a cake usually involves the combination of flour, sugar and moisture such as milk, beaten eggs or flavouring, with a shortening such as butter or margarine. In the oven, the starch in the flour will absorb the shortening and moisture and the mixture will become elastic.

Air in the cake mixture will expand in the oven, causing the cake to rise. Often a chemical raising agent such as baking powder is added, or self-raising flour with s raising agent is part of the recipe.

In most cakes, self-raising flour, that is, with a raising agent already added, is part of the recipe. However, some recipes may require stiffly beaten eggs, which will aerate the mixture. In this case, self-raising flour should not be used or the cake will rise rapidly then sink before it sets.

You can make your own self-raising flour by adding 1 teaspoon cream of tartar and ½ teaspoon bicarbonate of soda to 250 g plain flour, or by adding 2 teaspoons baking powder to the plain flour. Sift ingredients thoroughly.

The richer the cake and the longer the cooking, the thicker the paper lining should be on the tin to protect the cake from burning.

The best shortenings for cakes are butter and margarine. If you use lard, you will have to disguise the taste — for example with a strong spice.

Use caster, granulated white or granulated raw sugar in cakes unless the recipe stipulates otherwise.

Remember, brown sugar is lighter than white.

Beaten eggs are a good raising agent.

Make sure eggs are fresh before beating by breaking each one in to a cup separately.

Cakes — tips

Before you start making a cake, assemble all the ingredients and taste or test for freshness.

Sift dry ingredients twice to mix thoroughly and to make the cake mixture lighter.

When creaming butter and sugar, stand the basin in a sink of warm water. This will soften the butter and hasten the process, but do not let the butter get too soft and oily.

Use a wooden spoon or your hand to cream butter and sugar.

Cream butter and sugar until white and fluffy. This can take a few minutes, even in an electric beater.

Caster sugar will dissolve quicker than granulated sugar in butter and sugar blends.

Sometimes a recipe calls for the rubbing in method of combining shortening and sugar. Add the butter in small pieces to the sifted flour, and use your fingers and thumbs to rub flour and butter together making a crumbly mixture.

Try to incorporate plenty of air into the mixture by working with your hands above the bowl and letting the crumbs fall back in.

Do not let the heat of your hands make the mixture oily.

Bake small cakes near the top of the oven, larger and butter cakes in the middle, and very large and fruit cakes in the lower part of the oven.

A cake is cooked when it is golden brown and just beginning to shrink from the sides of the tin.

Also, a fine skewer inserted into the thickest part of the cake should come out dry and clean.

To test doneness with a metal skewer, warm the skewer first.

For sponges, if you press lightly with a finger in the centre of the cake the impression should disappear at once if it is cooked.

Turn sponges and small cakes out on a wire rack as soon as they are cooked. Leave large cakes in their tin for 10 minutes before carefully turning out.

If a cake is sticking to the tin, stand the bottom of the tin on a wet dishcloth for 2-3 minutes before turning it out.

Chocolate cake

This simple cake can be iced or simply sprinkled with desiccated coconut and icing sugar. There's no traditional creaming of butter and sugar but it has proved to be a family favourite.

Preheat the oven to 180°C. Place in the blender bowl 1 cup sifted self-raising flour, 2 generous tablespoons cocoa, 1 teaspoon vanilla essence, 1 cup sugar, ½ cup milk and 2 eggs. Melt 3 tablespoons butter or margarine and add. Beat the mixture really well on high speed for 3 minutes. Bake in a greased loaf tin for about 45 minutes.

Glazing

Glazing is brushing the top of pastry with a liquid to improve the appearance when cooked.

Glaze only the top surface of pastry, and apply the

glaze lightly just before baking.

Use milk or beaten egg and milk to glaze meat pies.

Use 1 tablespoon of sugar mixed with 1 tablespoon of water to glaze fruit pies.

Icing

Use this basic recipe and add vanilla or almond essence, cocoa, instant coffee, or lemon or orange juice to flavour it according to taste.

Put ¾ cup icing sugar in a bowl with a walnut of butter and the flavouring of your choice. Add sufficient boiling water, a tablespoon at a time, to make the mixture just spreadable.

Be careful not to add too much water. Icing sugar goes liquid very quickly.

Pastry

In pastry making, a dough is produced from flour and shortening — the best of all shortenings is butter as it gives a better flavour and is not as greasy as lard. Pastry should be as light as possible, and this depends on the amount of cold air incorporated into the mixture during the preparation of the dough.

Small pieces of softened butter are rubbed into plain flour with a pinch of salt added. A little cold water is added to make a dough.

This method will produce a shortcrust pastry, used for

lining quiches, tarts and flans, or to cover some pies. It may be sweetened if required for tartlets or mince pies.

A slightly different method is used to make light puff pastries. The butter is added to the flour through a process of rolling out the dough and folding it over small pieces of butter. This produces layers in the pastry and allows for more cold air to be incorporated so that it will rise in a hot oven.

Puff and flaky pastry is used for sweet or savoury pies, sausage rolls or vol-au-vents.

Pastry — choux
This is a deliciously different French pastry, more like a batter than a pastry, that is the shell for cream puffs and éclairs.

Preheat the oven to 220°C. Put 1 cup water and ½ cup butter into a saucepan and melt butter slowly, stirring. Bring to the boil, remove from the heat and add 1 cup sifted plain flour. Stir the mixture until it is smooth and forms a ball. Cool slightly. Add 3 eggs, one at a time, beating the mixture until smooth after each addition. Cool. Place tablespoons of mixture on a greased and floured oven tray and bake for about 15 minutes on set temperature, then reduce the heat to 180°C for 30 minutes.

Remove from the oven and cool on the tray.

Pierce puffs so that they will stay crisp. When cool fill with whipped sweetened cream.

Pastry — puff

When making puff and flaky pastry, make sure you keep the flakes or butter evenly spread through the dough during the rolling out process.

Here's a simple puff pastry recipe that you can use to cover a sweet or savoury pie. *See* the chapter on eggs for how to make an egg and bacon pie.

Sift 2 cups plain flour with a pinch of salt. Take ¾ cup butter (soft) and add to the flour in small pieces. Turn the butter in, but do not work it. Lightly mix in ¼

cup water and a few drops of lemon juice. Turn the mixture on to a floured board and shape into a flat rectangle. Sprinkle with a little flour, then fold the top and bottom of the rectangle over each other. Rest the pastry for a few minutes in the refrigerator, then sprinkle with flour and roll the pastry out lightly again. Rest it in the refrigerator. Repeat the flouring, folding and resting process twice more. Cover the pastry and refrigerate until needed.

You can also add a beaten egg yolk with the other liquid in this mixture for a richer glazed pastry.

Alternatively, glaze the top of your pie with beaten

whole egg or yolk before baking.

Roll the dough with quick even short strokes, lift the rolling pin up between strokes to allow air to circulate over the dough. This makes the layers in the pastry when it rises.

Pastry — shortcrust

Use your fingertips to rub the butter into the flour when you are making shortcrust pastry.

Lift your hands to allow the flour to fall back into the bowl. This will allow air to be incorporated into the mixture.

Use this basic shortcrust recipe for quiches and flan bases. If you add a tablespoon of caster sugar to the dry ingredients, it can be used as a sweet tart base. *See* the chapter on dairy products for how to make a simple quiche lorraine.

Remember, shortcrust pastry should have a crisp, rich texture when baked.

Take 1 cup plain flour sifted with a pinch of salt and add 2 tablespoons soft butter in small pieces. Work the mixture between your fingers until it is crumbly, then add $1\frac{1}{2}$ tablespoons cold water and work this in. Roll the mixture into a ball and refrigerate covered until you are ready to roll it out (at least 1 hour).

Pastry — tips

Cool hands and a cool atmosphere are essential for pastry making.

Work on a cool surface. A stone or marble bench is ideal.

Sprinkle cornflour on the bench to stop the dough from sticking.

Always sift the flour and salt together for a smooth result.

Mix in shortening and combine ingredients with a knife.

Don't use too much water — it will make the pastry hard.

Make sure your water is cold when you add it to the dough.

Do not overwork the dough or handle it too much. This will make the pastry tough.

You must have a hot oven to cook most pastry — at least 200°C. It is the heat that causes the dough to rise as the air in the mixture expands, and the shortening to melt and blend with the flour.

If the oven is not hot enough, you will have heavy, rubbery pastry.

After you have made dough, refrigerate it for 30 minutes or so before you use it to make a pie. This will reduce shrinkage